# THE FEMALE ATHLETE:
# Reach for Victory

*MATT BRZYCKI*
*JASON GALLUCCI*
*TOM KELSO*
*SAM KNOPIK*
*JOHN RINALDO*
*SCOTT SAVOR*

Wish Publishing
Terre Haute, Indiana
www.wishpublishing.com

Wish
PUBLISHING

LCCN: 2004118279

Book edited by Matt Brzycki
Cover designed by Phil Velikan
Cover photography by
Interior Photographs:
Jason Gallucci – all photographs in Chapters 1 and 2
Scott Savor – all photographs in Chapters 5 and 6
Pete Silletti – all other photographs

Printed in the United States of America
10 9 8 7 6 5 4 3 2 1

Published in the United States by
Wish Publishing
P.O. Box 10337
Terre Haute, Indiana 47801, USA
www.wishpublishing.com

Distributed in the United States by
Cardinal Publishers Group
Indianapolis, Indiana 46264

## DEDICATIONS

Matt Brzycki: *To my lovely wife, Alicia, and our darling son, Ryan. Thanks for being there.*

Jason Gallucci: *To my wife, Angelique, my son, Jason Gabriel, and my family whose love and support are my true inspiration.*

Tom Kelso: *To those in the strength/fitness industry who strive for sensible training plans, safe exercise protocols and truthful communication with their clientele.*

Samuel Knopik: *To Sarah, Emma, Maragreta and Kristin. They're the female athletes in my life who provide me with an abundance of inspiration each day. And to one of the most intense people I know, Jeff Roudebush. Thanks for showing me the way.*

John Rinaldo: *To Jenn Army for her friendship and inspiration.*

Scott Savor: *To my mother, Patty, my father, Dean, and my sister, Krista, for their continued love and support.*

## THANK YOU

Charity Bonfiglio who appears in numerous photographs in the book.

Cheri Drysdale who collected the data for the tables in Chapter 1.

Lisa Shall who appears in the photgaphs in Chapters 1 and 2.

Pete Silletti who took many of the photographs for the book.

Lori Wild, Melissa Harakas, Ryan Huntley and Lori Howard for their efforts and contributions to Chapters 5 and 6.

The National Collegiate Athletic Association (NCAA) Injury Surveillance System for providing data used in Chapter 7.

All athletic trainers who contributed to the success of the NCAA Injury Surveillance System.

# Table of Contents

# Foreword

The days of asking why female athletes should do strength training are a thing of the past. They do strength training because they are athletes. And athletes need to do strength training because of four key reasons: speed, strength, performance and injury prevention. All of these components are intertwined. You perform better when you are faster and stronger. You are faster when you aren't injured. If you are injured you can't perform. Strength enhances speed and endurance. And on and on. No longer will you hear a female athlete ask, "Will I get bigger?" Instead, you'll hear, "Will I get better?" And the answer is a resounding yes.

My first priority as a coach is not to win. My first priority is to keep my athletes healthy. Injuries will happen. You can't control every factor. But you can prepare.

We keep them healthy by designing a preseason training program that is going to prepare their bodies for the rigors of top competition. If athletes are pulling muscles, developing overuse injuries or incurring common injuries, you don't have to look any further than your conditioning and strength-training programs. These programs will keep the athletes in the game so that winning can become your priority. And that's the fun part! This book provides all of the information necessary to develop such a training program – the why, how and when for preparing yourself or your team.

We often use the saying "preparation breeds confidence." When you know that your body is prepared through proper conditioning and strength training, your entire game is elevated. There are so many variables in competition and so few things that you can truly control. This is a component that you can control. Strength, speed and fitness are measurable. You can determine your starting point and measure how much each area has improved. And the knowledge that you are stronger and fitter really does "breed confidence."

When asked "What's the difference between high school and college sports?" my answer is always "speed and strength." The best high school athletes are the ones who continue to play in college, so better skill and higher performance are inevitable. It's the speed and strength of the athletes that often separates the good from the great and, consequently, the average teams from the great teams. Sure, some athletes are already fast. And some are really strong. But it doesn't have to end there. Can you get stronger? Absolutely. Can you get faster? Absolutely. Will it improve your performance? There is no question. But you have to go about it correctly, with a solid understanding of what is needed and how to move forward. This book doesn't just tell you to do strength training and conditioning – it tells you *why* you should do strength training and conditioning and *how* to do them correctly. And it doesn't stop when you've reached your goal. Getting to the top is only fun if you stay there – this book tells you how.

Whether you are a high school sophomore soccer player or a middle-aged weekend golfer, the answers to improving your game and lengthening your career are in this book. It contains clear-cut, understandable methods to reach your "A" game. So dive into this book and "prepare" yourself for great things. Your competition is nervously waiting.

Beth Bozman
Head Field Hockey Coach
Duke University

# The Importance of Strength Training for the Female Athlete

*Jason Gallucci, M.S., S.C.C.C., C.S.C.S.*

While strength training seems to be a relatively new and in-vogue topic in today's society, its history can actually be traced back to Ancient Greek Mythology. However, even as late as the mid 1960s, strength training – or "weight training" as it was more commonly referred – was shunned by most of the athletic community in the United States. At this time, coaches believed that the risks of strength training greatly outweighed the potential benefits. During the same period, other countries – such as the former East Germany and former Soviet Union – were more advanced in the science of strength training and were producing superior athletes. It was the surge of success by these Eastern European athletes that prompted the massive growth of scientific studies regarding strength training in the United States. With this growth came a greater understanding of the physiology, anatomy and mechanics of the human body.

It was hardly a coincidence that at this time, strength-training equipment became more complex. Free weights were the primary tools in strength training along with primitive pulley systems. With greater understanding of the human body came more equipment. In the late 1960s, Arthur Jones was at the head of creating his Nautilus™line of equipment and completely rewrote the standards.

This is the groundwork that paved the relatively short road that strength training has come during the last four decades. Strength and conditioning coaches have become common in professional and amateur sports. Numerous theories of strength training have been developed as well as countless companies designing their own style of equipment. Still, today, there's no scientific evidence that proves there's one superior way to perform strength training. However, the benefits of a properly designed program have become clear.

Today, strength training has many benefits that far exceed any of its early expectations. The goal of this chapter is to illustrate how strength training can prove beneficial beyond increasing basic levels of strength. It should be noted that any program will only prove beneficial if it's physiologically sound and if the athlete who's training puts forth the effort necessary to achieve success.

## THE THREE MAIN GOALS OF STRENGTH TRAINING

The overall purpose of any strength-training program is to help an athlete achieve maximum athletic potential. In concurrence with the concepts that were mentioned by Michael Bradley in the first book of this series (*The Female Athlete: Train for Success*), there are three main goals of a strength-training program: injury prevention, physical development and mental development. To have a well-balanced athlete that will be truly prepared for peak performance, all three of these concepts must be addressed within a given training protocol.

## Injury Prevention

If you analyze the big picture, it's easy to see why injury prevention is the most important concept to consider when designing a strength-training program. While physical and mental potential can be enhanced with strength training, peak potential will never be realized if an athlete isn't able to practice or compete in a given sport. Consider a sport-specific example of a basketball center who wants to become more proficient at rebounding. Proper strength training can increase the athlete's potential but strength training alone will not make her a better basketball player. To become better at rebounding a basketball, the athlete must practice rebounding a basketball. This seems to be common sense and it is. A properly designed strength-training program is a stepping stone but, ultimately, rebounding or jumping is a specific skill. It's a skill that will only get better with practice. Therefore, the primary goal should be to keep an athlete healthy so that she can practice and, more importantly, compete at a high level.

To help prevent injuries, a biomechanical analysis should be performed for a specific sport. Once this is done, the main areas of concern will become clear. These areas should be the primary focus of an athlete's training program. Take the basketball center again, for example. The sport of basketball requires an athlete to run, jump and change directions rapidly on a surface that's unforgiving at best. In this case, the primary areas of concern would be the lower back along with the knee and ankle joints. Here, the potential risk of injury can be lowered by choosing exercises that focus on the muscle groups involved in the movements of these joints. For a comprehensive injury analysis of a collegiate basketball team and soccer team, refer to Tables 1.1 and 1.2, respectively. The information presented in these tables is based upon subjective observations made by a certified university athletic trainer during one team's competitive season in each sport. Understand that these data are presented for coaching purposes and not as scientific research. It's important that you know your population and train them accordingly.

If your goal is to decrease the occurrence of injury in the athletic arena, then it's imperative that you don't cause or increase the risk of injury with your training. To do this, there are some fundamental truths to strength training that must be applied.

| INJURIES | 2001-02 | | | 2002-03 | | |
|---|---|---|---|---|---|---|
| | TOTAL NUMBER | PRACTICES MISSED | GAMES MISSED | TOTAL NUMBER | PRACTICES MISSED | GAMES MISSED |
| *Head/Face* | 4 | 4 | 3 | 8 | 16 | 4 |
| Concussion | 2 | 4 | 3 | 2 | 16 | 4 |
| Eye Abrasion | 0 | 0 | 0 | 1 | 0 | 0 |
| Facial Contusion | 0 | 0 | 0 | 2 | 0 | 0 |
| Facial Laceration | 2 | 0 | 0 | 1 | 0 | 0 |
| Teeth | 0 | 0 | 0 | 0 | 0 | 0 |
| Nose Bleed/Contusion | 0 | 0 | 0 | 2 | 0 | 0 |
| *Shoulder* | 0 | 0 | 0 | 0 | 0 | 0 |
| *Forearm/Elbow* | 2 | 1 | 2 | 0 | 0 | 0 |
| Elbow Contusion | 1 | 0 | 0 | 0 | 0 | 0 |
| Elbow Sprain | 1 | 1 | 2 | 0 | 0 | 0 |
| *Wrist/Hand* | 4 | 0 | 0 | 4 | 0 | 0 |
| Tendinitis | 1 | 0 | 0 | 0 | 0 | 0 |
| Wrist Sprain | 0 | 0 | 0 | 1 | 0 | 0 |
| Wrist Fracture | 0 | 0 | 0 | 0 | 0 | 0 |
| Thumb Sprain | 1 | 0 | 0 | 3 | 0 | 0 |
| Finger Sprain | 1 | 0 | 0 | 0 | 0 | 0 |
| Finger Fracture | 1 | 0 | 0 | 0 | 0 | 0 |
| *Ribs/Chest* | 0 | 0 | 0 | 3 | 1 | 1 |
| Rib Contusion | 0 | 0 | 0 | 1 | 0 | 0 |
| Rib Dysfunction | 0 | 0 | 0 | 1 | 0 | 0 |
| Chest Pain | 0 | 0 | 0 | 1 | 1 | 1 |
| *Lower Back/Pelvis* | 8 | 22 | 8 | 1 | 0 | 0 |
| Low-Back Dysfunction | 3 | 20 | 8 | 1 | 0 | 0 |
| Low-Back Contusion | 1 | 0 | 0 | 0 | 0 | 0 |
| Muscular Spasms | 0 | 0 | 0 | 0 | 0 | 0 |
| Disc | 1 | 2 | 0 | 0 | 0 | 0 |
| Pelvis Dysfunction | 3 | 0 | 0 | 0 | 0 | 0 |
| *Thigh/Groin* | 2 | 0 | 0 | 2 | 3 | 1 |
| Hip Flexor Strain | 1 | 0 | 0 | 0 | 0 | 0 |
| Hamstring Strain | 1 | 0 | 0 | 0 | 0 | 0 |
| Quadricep Strain | 0 | 0 | 0 | 1 | 3 | 1 |
| Groin Strain | 0 | 0 | 0 | 1 | 0 | 0 |
| *Knee* | 1 | 0 | 0 | 1 | 0 | 0 |
| Tendinitis | 1 | 0 | 0 | 1 | 0 | 0 |
| ACL | 0 | 0 | 0 | 0 | 0 | 0 |
| *Lower Leg* | 1 | 0 | 0 | 1 | 0 | 0 |
| Shin Splints | 0 | 0 | 0 | 1 | 0 | 0 |
| Calf | 0 | 0 | 0 | 0 | 0 | 0 |
| Stress Fracture | 0 | 0 | 0 | 0 | 0 | 0 |
| Contusion | 1 | 0 | 0 | 0 | 0 | 0 |

**TABLE 1.1: BASKETBALL INJURY ANALYSIS** (reprinted with permission of Cheri Drysdale, ATC), continued on following page.

| INJURIES | 2001-02 (cont.) | | | 2002-03 (cont.) | | |
|---|---|---|---|---|---|---|
| | TOTAL NUMBER | PRACTICES MISSED | GAMES MISSED | TOTAL NUMBER | PRACTICES MISSED | GAMES MISSED |
| *Foot/Ankle* | *6* | *4* | *0* | *12* | *74* | *12* |
| Ankle Sprain | 5 | 4 | 0 | 6 | 8 | 1 |
| Plantar Fascitis | 0 | 0 | 0 | 0 | 0 | 0 |
| Heel Bursitis | 1 | 0 | 1 | 0 | 0 | 0 |
| Sesamoiditis | 0 | 0 | 0 | 2 | 0 | 0 |
| Stress Fracture | 0 | 0 | 0 | 3 | 65 | 11 |
| Toe Fracture | 0 | 0 | 0 | 1 | 1 | 0 |
| *Mononucleosis/Illness* | *1* | *2* | *0* | *4* | *24* | *0* |
| TOTALS | 29 | 33 | 13 | 36 | 118 | 18 |

**TABLE 1.1 (CONT.): BASKETBALL INJURY ANALYSIS** (reprinted with permission of Cheri Drysdale, ATC).

| INJURIES | 2001 | | | 2002 | | |
|---|---|---|---|---|---|---|
| | TOTAL NUMBER | PRACTICES MISSED | GAMES MISSED | TOTAL NUMBER | PRACTICES MISSED | GAMES MISSED |
| *Head/Face* | *5* | *4* | *1* | *4* | *3* | *1* |
| Concussion | 1 | 1 | 0 | 2 | 2 | 1 |
| Head Contusion | 1 | 0 | 0 | 0 | 0 | 0 |
| Eye Contusion | 2 | 3 | 1 | 0 | 0 | 0 |
| Ear Drum | 0 | 0 | 0 | 1 | 1 | 0 |
| Teeth | 0 | 0 | 0 | 1 | 0 | 0 |
| Nose Bleed/Contusion | 1 | 0 | 0 | 0 | 0 | 0 |
| *Shoulder* | *2* | *3* | *1* | *1* | *0* | *0* |
| AC Sprain | 0 | 0 | 0 | 1 | 0 | 0 |
| Subluxation | 1 | 3 | 1 | 0 | 0 | 0 |
| Contusion | 1 | 0 | 0 | 0 | 0 | 0 |
| *Forearm/Elbow* | *0* | *0* | *0* | *0* | *0* | *0* |
| *Wrist/Hand* | *0* | *0* | *0* | *3* | *0* | *0* |
| Tendinitis | 0 | 0 | 0 | 2 | 0 | 0 |
| Thumb Sprain | 0 | 0 | 0 | 1 | 0 | 0 |
| *Ribs/Chest* | *0* | *0* | *0* | *0* | *0* | *0* |
| *Lower Back/Pelvis* | *4* | *2* | *0* | *1* | *1* | *0* |
| Upper-Back Dysfunction | 1 | 1 | 0 | 0 | 0 | 0 |
| Lower-Back Dysfunction | 3 | 1 | 0 | 1 | 0 | 0 |
| *Thigh/Groin* | *10* | *13* | *2* | *4* | *1* | *0* |
| Hip Flexor Strain | 2 | 3 | 0 | 0 | 0 | 0 |
| Hip Contusion | 0 | 0 | 0 | 1 | 0 | 0 |
| Hamstring Strain | 5 | 6 | 1 | 2 | 1 | 0 |
| Quadricep Strain | 2 | 3 | 1 | 0 | 0 | 0 |
| Quadricep Contusion | 1 | 1 | 0 | 0 | 0 | 0 |
| Groin Strain | 0 | 0 | 0 | 1 | 0 | 0 |
| *Knee* | *4* | *9* | *1* | *6* | *7* | *0* |
| IT Band Syndrome | 0 | 0 | 0 | 1 | 3 | 0 |
| Patello-Femoral Syndrome | 1 | 3 | 1 | 1 | 0 | 0 |
| Patella Subluxation | 0 | 0 | 0 | 1 | 3 | 0 |
| Hyperextension | 1 | 0 | 0 | 2 | 1 | 0 |
| Contusion | 0 | 0 | 0 | 1 | 0 | 0 |
| MCL Sprain | 1 | 3 | 0 | 0 | 1 | 0 |
| Laceration | 1 | 3 | 0 | 0 | 1 | 0 |
| *Foot/Ankle* | *14* | *15* | *2* | *9* | *15* | *3* |
| Ankle Sprain | 12 | 12 | 1 | 6 | 10 | 1 |
| Foot/Arch Sprain | 2 | 3 | 1 | 0 | 0 | 0 |
| Tendinitis | 0 | 0 | 0 | 2 | 2 | 2 |
| Toe Sprain | 0 | 0 | 0 | 1 | 3 | 0 |
| *Mononucleosis/Illness* | *6* | *21* | *4* | *4* | *11* | *3* |
| TOTALS | 45 | 67 | 11 | 32 | 37 | 7 |

TABLE 1.2: SOCCER INJURY ANALYSIS (reprinted with permission of Cheri Drysdale, ATC)

## Balance

When designing a program, it's critical to balance the workload across the joints. Overtraining a certain muscle group while neglecting another one can lead to an altered posture or gait which will inevitably lead to injury through decreased flexibility or increased stress on the bones or joints. A simple way to ensure balance in a program is to follow a push-pull method. Simply stated, for every "pushing" exercise you do, perform a "pulling" exercise that incorporates the same joints. For instance, if you perform a set of bench press (a "pushing" exercise) for 8 - 12 repetitions, follow that with a set of seated row (a "pulling" exercise") for 8 - 12 repetitions. There are exceptions to the rule so a functional knowledge of anatomy will prove beneficial. (To avoid confusion, it's important to note that all muscles "pull" when they contract; however, muscle contractions cause joints to extend and flex which produce movements that can be described as either "pushing" or "pulling.")

## Warm-up

According to Wilmore and Costill (1994), "A warm-up period will increase both heart rate and breathing, preparing you for the efficient and safe functioning of your heart, blood vessels, lungs, and muscles during the more vigorous exercise that follows." The authors add, "A good warm-up also reduces the amount of muscle and joint soreness that you experience during the early stages of the exercise program and can decrease your risk of injury." In recent years, dynamic warm-ups that include exercises that focus on specific movements have become increasingly popular. As preparation for a bench press, such a warm-up might include push-ups and shoulder rotations (just to name a few movements). Regardless of how the warm-up is performed, if done properly, it will increase the muscle's ability to perform work while decreasing the risk of injury.

## Proper Technique

One of the earliest concerns regarding strength training was that it was believed to decrease an athlete's flexibility. This is a legitimate concern if training is performed improperly. Using a limited range of motion in any exercise has the potential to shorten the muscle-belly length and, therefore, decrease flexibility. It's critical that an athlete train a muscle group, regardless of the exercise, through a full but safe range of motion. A safe range of motion implies that there's no overstretching of the muscle-tendon complex or ligaments involved in the movement. Teaching an athlete to keep a constant load on her muscle and to control the movement will assist in creating a safer training environment.

## Physical Development

In the past, absolute strength levels (or force production) have been the focus of the majority of strength and conditioning programs. Today, especially with a female athlete, strength-training programs incorporate specific abilities that are essential in the development of any athletic skill. Abilities such as balance, coordination, power, speed and agility as well as an enhanced neuromuscular response to stress can all be addressed through proper training.

## Force Production

The body is an intricate system that was designed to recognize and adjust to external stresses that are placed upon it. One of the key concepts of a successful strength-training program is based upon the method of progressive overload. Essentially, you're asking your muscles to do more than they could the last week or the week before either by increasing the repetitions completed or increasing the weight lifted. When implementing a traditional high-intensity training (HIT) protocol, a double progression is utilized. During this style of training, every set is typically performed to momentary muscular exhaustion – or what's commonly referred to as "failure" – and progression is dependent upon a prescribed repetition range (such as 8 - 12). In this case, there's a double progression because to increase weight on an exercise, an athlete must first be able to increase the number of repetitions that she can perform with a specific weight. So as properly performed repetitions increase, so will the resistance (weight).

The body has distinct methods of overcoming this stress which are primarily contingent upon the experience level of the athlete. When an athlete first begins a strength-training program, most of the improvements are related to an increased proficiency of the neuromuscular system. This system is extremely efficient in the human body as it will recruit and activate only those muscle fibers that are necessary to perform a certain task. This was originally documented by Dr. Elwood Henneman and has since been referred to as the "Henneman size principle of motor-unit recruitment." Simply stated, the neuromuscular system contains two types of motor units – small and large – that activate slow- and fast-twitch muscle fibers, respectively. When small forces are needed, only the smaller motor units are activated. As the forces become greater, the larger units are activated (Henneman 1957). According to Zatsiorsky (1995), maximal muscular force is exerted when three things occur: (1) the maximal number of motor units is recruited; (2) rate coding is optimal (frequency of motoneuron excitation); and (3) the motor units are activated synchronously. However, that's a learned effect and untrained athletes can only activate a percentage of those motor units often at slower, unsynchronized rates. During the initial phases of strength training, the neuromuscular system becomes more proficient in all three of the aforementioned areas essentially because the central nervous system becomes more effective at communicating with the targeted muscle groups. As an athlete learns to recruit more muscle fibers at a quicker, more synchronized rate, they can produce more force. Therefore, the gains seen during the early stages of strength training typically aren't due to any structural changes of the muscle but rather in the body's unique communication system.

Approximately four weeks after the start of a strength-training program, the neuromuscular system will be working much more effectively and the body will have to find a new way to overcome the stresses of progressive overload. At this point, structural changes to the size and shape of muscles will begin to occur assuming that the athlete is training with a proper level of intensity, incorporating a healthy diet and getting enough recovery. A muscle of greater mass contains more of the contractile proteins (actin and myosin) that are essential in force development. The most widely accepted theory of how resistance training leads to increased lean-muscle mass is through muscular hypertrophy. The term "muscular hypertrophy" refers to an increase in the size of a muscle at the cellular level that's usually due to an increased number of contractile proteins within the myofibrils of the muscle. The greater the number of contractile proteins in a muscle, the more force it can produce. As a result, a muscle of greater cross-sectional area (or size) can produce more force than a muscle of smaller cross-sectional area.

A properly designed program must take into consideration the needs of the specific sport. Most women don't have the genetic potential to increase the size of their muscles to a significant degree. Even if this were possible, it wouldn't be advantageous for women to be excessively muscular in most sports. It should also be noted that resistance training and cardiovascular training decrease body fat at a greater rate than cardiovascular training alone. Increased levels of body fat are directly related to decreased force-producing abilities.

## Coordination

As mentioned previously, it's critical that the central nervous system is able to communicate with the targeted muscle groups to produce force. The same concept also applies to muscle groups that communicate with other muscle groups through an intricate feedback system. This inter-muscular communication is known as "proprioception." When performing exercises that involve movement across more than one joint, multiple muscle groups are activated. These muscle groups lengthen or shorten depending upon the joint action with which it's involved. Therefore, muscles must learn to communicate with each other when performing a task that involves multiple-joint movements. Figure 1.1 shows an athlete performing a walking lunge with her bodyweight.

**FIGURE 1.1: WALKING LUNGE (Photo by Jason Gallucci)**

During this exercise, there's movement at the hip, knee and ankle joints. Every major muscle below the trunk is active at some point during this exercise. The

ability of an athlete to successfully perform this exercise is very much dependant upon the communicative capabilities of the muscles that are activated.
Much like discussed earlier, this system becomes more efficient with repetition. This ability is something that, hopefully, will transfer – albeit indirectly –
to specific athletic movements as they mostly involve simultaneous multiple-
joint actions.

## Balance

It stands to reason if exercises that involve multiple joints enhance an
athlete's proprioceptive skills, balance may also be improved. This is especially
true when exercises are chosen where an athlete is asked to move while standing. In no way does this minimize the importance of single-joint movements or
machine exercises as gains in absolute strength can improve an athlete's ability
to stabilize her body during more complex exercises. An exercise such as a single-
leg squat on an 18-inch box – shown in Figures 1.2 and 1.3 – is an example of a
great strength exercise for the muscles of the hip and thigh that also places a
focus on the development of balance.

**FIGURE 1.2: SINGLE-LEG
SQUAT, FRONT VIEW
(Photo by Jason Gallucci)**

**FIGURE 1.3: SINGLE-LEG
SQUAT, SIDE VIEW
(Photo by Jason Gallucci)**

## Power and Speed

If work is defined as "force times distance" and power as "work divided
by time," then power can be defined as "force times distance divided by time."
Therefore, an athlete's ability to generate power is dependent upon two criteria. The first is the relative strength level of the athlete or how much force an
athlete can produce against a given resistance. The second is the rate at which
an athlete can produce that force. With strength training, the ability to produce

force is increased. If the force-production capabilities of the lower body are increased at a greater rate than body mass, the relative strength of the lower body has been enhanced (the given resistance being body mass). In this case, an athlete will have a greater potential to move her body while running, jumping or performing any athletic movement on her feet. As mentioned earlier, the rate at which an athlete can produce force will be improved by enhancing neuromuscular control as a result of strength training as well as practicing specific tasks in the arena which they compete. When training for power, an athlete doesn't have to train fast in the weight room. During concentric contractions (muscle shortening), greater forces are produced at slower angular velocities. This will be discussed in much greater detail in the next chapter (on sport biomechanics).

## Agility

Agility refers to an athlete's ability to control her body in space, usually during tasks that require quick changes of direction or body position. The underlying components of agility are speed, coordination and balance. As strength training can enhance all of those components, it can also lead to an increased potential during agility exercises or sport tasks that require quick changes of direction. Over the years, strength training has become much more "functional" for athletes. Today, it's common to see the use of agility ladders, cones and other devices that were designed to enhance an athlete's ability to control her body in space and thus increase her athletic potential.

## Mental Development

In all sports – with the possible exception of competitive weightlifting – there's a distinct difference between strength training and practicing. Results from strength training can be easily quantified while improvements in sport-specific skills are more challenging to measure on a daily basis. More often than not, coaches arbitrarily gauge improvement of specific skills. So, improvement can be measured from week to week, month to month and year to year. When strength training, an athlete is essentially asked to complete challenges or tasks. On a daily basis, there will always be success and failure. Over a period of time, however, an athlete should see a noticeable progression and, ultimately, success on all exercises.

Strength training teaches an athlete that success doesn't come easy and that sacrifices must be made for increased performance. Success in training will only come if an athlete is disciplined in every aspect of her training. The most obvious aspect is making an athlete understand the effort that she must put forth to achieve success. On preparing his team for competition, Hall-of-Fame coach Vince Lombardi once said "The harder you work, the harder it is to surrender." There are countless clichés that can be used but they all boil down to the same concept: An athlete must prepare her body to succeed and, in doing so, she'll gain the confidence that will allow her to reach her potential.

Strength training can also be utilized as an invaluable educational tool with regard to proper nutrition. This has become increasingly important, especially with female athletes. Unfortunately, society reinforces poor dietary habits that can easily distort any athlete's perspective of her body image. As mentioned previously, proper nutrition is crucial to success in athletics and in physical development from strength training. An athlete should be educated about the fuels that her body needs to function at high levels. The fad diets of today aren't focused on improving an individual's health; rather, they're focused on improving an individual's body image. A low-carbohydrate diet, for example, may help an athlete lose weight and improve her body image. But remember, carbohydrates are the only fuel source that the body can use during anaerobic (or intense) activity. Since most sports are anaerobic by nature, it's easy to see how a low-carbohydrate diet can adversely affect athletic performance. It's fortunate that as strength training has become more popular with female athletes, there are more positive role models on the professional and collegiate levels who promote both a healthy diet and a positive body image.

## FINAL THOUGHTS

Strength and conditioning has become a vital component for training a female athlete to be more competitive in any sport. In review, the most important role of a strength-training program is to keep an athlete healthy throughout the season. An athlete's health should never be compromised by any exercise in the weight room that could be immediately harmful or increase the chance of injury in the future. It's always wise to warm up prior to performing any strength training and choose exercises that allow constant loading on the muscle through a full, safe range of motion.

It's also important to understand the sport for which an athlete is training. Different sports place different demands upon athletes. Understanding these demands will help an athlete determine which type of exercises on which to focus. For instance, a hockey player would want to make sure that she devotes some time to single-leg exercises that incorporate balance and coordination. Utilizing such exercises will also add variety to the training program and help keep an athlete motivated to train with a desirable level of effort.

Finally, keep in mind that intensity is the key to improvement in the weight room. Don't get fooled into believing that if an athlete spends a lot of time in the weight room then she's getting better. In the weight room, *quality* is much more important than *quantity*. If an athlete becomes bored during a training session or feels as if the session is dragging, her results will begin to diminish. The harder that an athlete trains, the shorter the session should be.

## REFERENCES

Henneman, E. 1957. Relation between size of neurons and their susceptibility to discharge. *Science* 126 (3287): 1345-1347.

Wilmore, J. H., and D. L. Costill. 1994. *Physiology of sport and exercise*. Champaign, IL: Human Kinetics Publishing, Inc., 524-525.

Zatsiorsky, V. M. 1995. *Science and practice of strength training*. Champaign, IL: Human Kinetics Publishing, Inc., 77-80.

# 2

# A Practical Approach to Sport Biomechanics

*Jason Gallucci, M.S., S.C.C.C., C.S.C.S.*

The study of sport biomechanics as it applies to the human body is much like the role that the study of architecture has in building a house or automotive engineering has in designing a car. Essentially, sport biomechanics is the study of human-body engineering. Since the early 1990s, much has been made of the advances that biomechanics has brought upon sport. It has become increasingly obvious that performance can be enhanced, not only by training with a high level of effort but also by training properly and using the appropriate tools. Basically, sport biomechanics is used to teach an athlete how to utilize her energy efficiently. It's also used to design equipment that will optimize performance by enhancing the tools that are utilized during a specific sport. Examples such as teaching a gymnast how to generate twist while airborne and designing golf clubs that enable an athlete to hit the ball farther and straighter are just a few ways that biomechanists have been improving sport performance. While it takes money to purchase the top-of-the-line equipment, it only takes a basic conceptual understanding of biomechanics to improve the quality of an athlete's training. This chapter will explain some basic principles of biomechanics and describe how these principles apply to designing a strength-training program.

## MUSCULAR ANATOMY

As stated previously, biomechanics is the study of human movement. To study movement of the human body, it's important to understand the basics of muscular anatomy. Additionally, the physiology of movement – such as enzyme control – is important. But for the purposes of keeping this discussion concise, it's assumed that the endocrine system is functioning normally and, therefore, can be ignored. Also keep in mind that there are three types of muscle found in the human body: skeletal, smooth and cardiac. Throughout this chapter, any reference to muscular function can be assumed to be that of skeletal muscle as this is the only type of muscle over which an individual has voluntary control.

To understand how the anatomy of a muscle affects movement, a single muscle cell – known as a "muscle fiber" – must be examined. A single muscle fiber can contain thousands of contractile elements that are known as "myofibrils." It's within the myofibril that the true functional unit of muscle is found:

the sarcomere. A schematic of a single sarcomere can be seen in Figure 2.1. This figure illustrates the two protein filaments – actin (the thin line) and myosin (the thick line) – that are primarily responsible for muscular contraction. It should be noted that Figure 2.1 shows a sarcomere in a resting (or inactive) state. While at rest, there's some crossover of the actin and myosin filaments that are shown within the A band. Within the A band, there's a region that contains only the thicker myosin filaments in the resting state. This is referred to as the "H zone" and it's where the M band is found.

In the late 1950s, Huxley proposed his sliding-filament model that's still widely accepted to this day as the theory of muscular contraction. Over time, his theory has been reviewed and modified but the fundamental principles remain the same. According to Huxley (1957), the thicker myosin filaments form cross-bridges via what has come to be called "myosin heads" (which are found in multiple at the ends of each myosin filament) with specific receptor sites on the thinner actin filaments. At this point, the myosin heads pull the actin filaments and cause them to slide closer to the M band, thus shortening the H zone. In a fully contracted muscle, the H zone will not be noticeable. Upon muscular relaxation, the cross-bridging of actin and myosin ceases and the protein filaments return to their inactive state. That's muscular contraction in its most uncomplicated form. It's important to realize that voluntary human movement is caused by muscular contraction and, as a result, the sarcomere plays an active role in every concept that's discussed in this chapter.

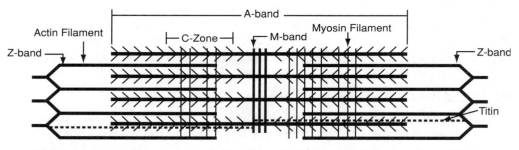

**FIGURE 2.1: SCHEMATIC OF A SINGLE SARCOMERE, THE FUNCTIONING UNIT OF SKELETAL MUSCLE. (Reprinted by permission of P. Luther, Imperial College of London, 2003.)**

## THE MECHANICS OF STRENGTH TRAINING

With an understanding of the contractile element, some of the parameters that affect its function can be discussed and, therefore, begin to shape training to maximize productivity. To begin, the following definitions should be clarified to eliminate any misunderstandings or misconceptions:

*Velocity* is the displacement or change in position divided by time (or, in shorthand, v = d/t).

*Acceleration* is the rate of change in velocity as a function of time (a = v/t). Since joint action occurs in an angular fashion, angular acceleration will be discussed.

*Force* is mass times acceleration (f = ma). This is Newton's Second Law of Motion (assuming that the mass of a body remains constant). Scientifically, force is measured in Newtons (N).

*Moment* is force times the moment arm of the force. This is Newton's Second Law of Motion applied to angular motion. The moment arm of the force is the length of a perpendicular drawn from the muscle-tendon complex to the axis of rotation of the joint.

*Strength* can be defined as "the maximum amount of force that a muscle or group of muscles can produce." It's often represented as a one-repetition maximum (1-RM) whether tested or estimated.

*Power* is force times distance divided by time (fd/t). Just as acceleration is a component of force, it's also a component of power. For the purposes of this chapter, the unit of measure for power will be foot-pounds per second (ft-lb/sec).

*Fast-twitch (FT) muscle fibers* are those that produce more force than slow-twitch muscle fibers but with less resistance to fatigue.

*Slow-twitch (ST) muscle fibers* are those that produce less force than fast-twitch muscle fibers but with more resistance to fatigue.

*Kinetic energy* is the energy that a body possesses due to its motion.

*Potential energy* is the energy that a body possesses due to its position.

*Contractile element* is the muscle and its force-producing properties (force-velocity, force-length and activation dynamics) when modeling muscle dynamics.

## ACTIVATION DYNAMICS

The force that a contractile element can produce is dependant upon the length of the muscle fibers, the velocity of the contraction and the active state of the muscle. The active state of the muscle represents the recruitment as well as the firing rate of the muscle fibers. Under normal conditions, the recruitment of muscle fibers follows a standard order that's based upon the size and rate of contraction (Henneman 1957). When a muscle fiber is recruited to produce force, it will increase its rate of firing as the level of effort increases. The number of fibers that are recruited and the rate at which they fire are the two neurological variables that determine muscular force (Stein, Zehr and Bobet 2000).

There are several simple implications that this has upon how to properly train an athlete for competition. The driving force behind both components of the active state of the muscle – recruitment and firing rate – is effort. There's a myth in strength training that to be fast on the athletic field, an athlete has to train fast in the weight room. The speed of movement isn't the key; rather, it's the *intent* to move the weight fast that's important. The body will recruit only those muscle fibers that are necessary to perform a task, regardless of the speed of movement.

So the goal in training must be to recruit the maximum amount of muscle fibers during each exercise. To accomplish this, two things must occur: First, an athlete must perform exercises where such an effort will be safe; second, an athlete must exert a maximum amount of effort. Understand that "a maximum amount of effort" doesn't necessarily mean lifting the heaviest weight possible for one repetition. (In fact, doing so is strongly discouraged for young female athletes.) Indeed, "a maximum amount of effort" could mean lifting the heaviest weight possible for 8 - 12 repetitions. When using a repetition scheme such as this, less weight must be used. This leads to another misconception. No anatomy book contains a picture of a muscle with a pair of eyes, meaning that a muscle has no idea what weight is being lifted. It only responds to the *intent* to lift the weight and the *effort* that must be put forth. The only way to ensure that the maximum amount of muscle fibers is being recruited is when a muscle

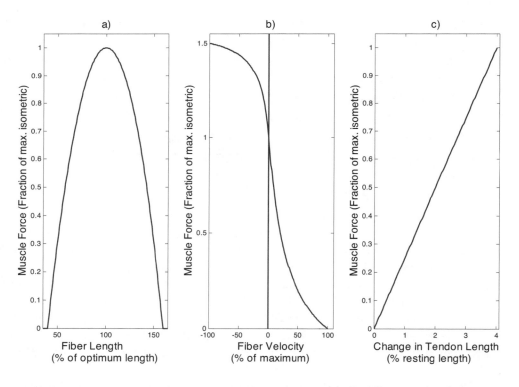

**FIGURE 2.2: THE KEY PROPERTIES OF THE MUSCLE MODEL. a) normalized force-length properties; b) normalized force-velocity properties; and c) tendon force-length curve. Note that muscle-fiber shortening (concentric muscle action), has been designated as a positive velocity.**

is trained to fatigue (or "failure") with a program that utilizes a system of progressive overload. This means all muscle fibers – including fast-twitch fibers – will be recruited during a set that uses controlled repetitions. As a side note, there's also a time delay of about 0.2 seconds between maximum neural excitation and maximum active state of muscle (Pandy, Anderson and Hull 1992). Stated otherwise, it takes a muscle about 0.2 seconds to generate maximum force after maximum excitation of the motoneurons. Training with controlled repetitions that emphasize the eccentric (negative) component of the lift helps to "prime" a muscle for the concentric (positive) phase of the exercise. This will allow a muscle to produce a greater amount of force as well as protect the associated joint from excessive stress.

## FORCE-LENGTH PROPERTIES OF MUSCLE

The force that a muscle fiber can produce changes with the length of the fibers. Figure 2.2a illustrates the relationship of muscular force (as a fraction of maximum isometric force) and muscle-fiber length (as a percentage of optimal length) as modeled by Challis (1999). By definition, when a muscle fiber is at optimal length, it will produce maximal force. This can be seen in the bell-shaped curve of Figure 2.2a. At values less than optimal length (contraction), force production is reduced because the cross-bridges are so tight that they interfere with each other; at values greater than optimal length, force production is also reduced because there's less overlap of the actin and myosin filaments so some cross-bridges cannot form.

Kulig, Andrews and Hay (1984) published a comprehensive review of the force-length relationship of various muscles and determined that when plotting force versus length (as a measure of joint angle as opposed to optimum length which is used in Figure 2.2a), the curves fell under three categories:

1. Ascending curves represented muscles that produced more force as the joint angle increased.

2. Descending curves represented muscles that produced less force as the joint angles decreased.

3. Ascending-descending curves represented muscles that initially produced more force as the joint angle increased but then produced less force as the joint angle continued to increase.

The force-length properties of a muscle fiber become slightly more complicated when considering muscles that cross two joints (which are known as "bi-articular muscles"). When a muscle crosses two joints, changing the angle of one joint will have an effect on the muscle's force-producing capabilities at the other joint simply because the length of the muscle fibers has been altered. A study by Gallucci and Challis (2002) evaluated the effects that two different ankle angles had on isokinetic knee flexion at 30, 75 and 150 degrees/second. (An isokinetic exercise is one where the velocity of movement is constant throughout the range of motion.) By altering the ankle angle from a fully dorsiflexed position (toes pointed up) to a fully plantar-flexed position (toes pointed down), the length of the bi-articular gastrocnemius was either lengthened or shortened, respectively. While the gastrocnemius is more commonly thought to perform plantar flexion, it also contributes to knee flexion (essentially a leg curl) as it crosses the knee joint. The results of the study showed that by fixing the ankle in dorsi flexion – and, thus, increasing the length of the gastrocnemius – significantly greater moments were found about the knee joint at all three angular velocities. From a practical standpoint, this proves that when the ankle was dorsi flexed, the gastrocnemius was operating at a more favorable point on its force-length curve than it was when the muscle was shortened in plantar flexion. The bottom line is that the athlete was stronger in that position.

When determining the modality of an exercise, it's important to understand the differences in the distinctive force-length curves of different muscles. While free weights offer certain advantages, properly designed machines are intended to match the strength curves of the targeted muscle. When using free weights, the amount of resistance that can be lifted is limited to the weakest joint angle of the movement (which is commonly referred to as the "sticking point"). A well-designed machine has variable resistance throughout the range of motion so the training effect isn't limited within the range of motion. This is not to say that an athlete should train exclusively on machines since there are some disadvantages that are associated with them. For one thing, machines operate through a fixed path that doesn't permit the body to rely heavily upon the stabilizing muscles during an exercise. It's these muscles that are critical in balance, coordination and, in most cases, joint stability.

Recently, training with bands and/or chains has also become extremely popular. Both of these methods are based upon the concept of variable resistance. An un-stretched band or a chain that rests on the floor offers no resistance. But as the band is stretched or the chain is lifted off the ground, the resistance increases. There are some advantages of this style of training. The main advantage is that there's typically less resistance throughout the range of motion when there would normally be more stress on the joints. If an athlete used bands to squat, for example, the resistance would decrease as the athlete squatted lower. It's the bottom phase of a squat where the joint pressure is the greatest on the knees and the lower back. However, the use of bands or chains is a gross oversimplification of the complex force-length curves of muscles, especially during an exercise such as a squat that incorporates many muscle groups with varying strength curves. Increases in muscular strength occur specifically at the joint angle at which they're trained (plus or minus several degrees). The use of bands and chains cannot be productive in fully taxing the muscle through a full range of motion. So while these devices can be valuable tools in the training of an athlete, they shouldn't be the only methods. Every method of training – regardless of how unconventional they may seem – can be useful tools in training athletes. Keep in mind that safety is of the utmost importance and that variety is essential to keep an athlete stimulated both physically as well as mentally.

## FORCE-VELOCITY PROPERTIES OF MUSCLE

As noted before, force production changes as the length of a muscle changes. Force production also changes as the *rate* of muscle-fiber length changes. This is considered the muscle-fiber force-velocity curve and it's pictured in Figure 2.2b. The force-velocity relationship of muscle fibers during shortening can be modeled using an equation developed by Hill (1938); the force-velocity relationship of muscle fibers during lengthening can be modeled using an equation from the work of Fitzhugh (1977). For these equations, muscle-fiber shortening has a positive velocity while muscle-fiber lengthening has a negative velocity. The research of Fitzhugh (1977) also shows that maximum eccentric (lengthening) force is 150% of the maximum isometric force. (An isometric contraction is a muscular contraction in which the joint angle doesn't change.) Figure 2.2b shows that as the velocity of contraction increases during a concentric motion (muscle-fiber shortening), the force-producing capability of the muscle fibers decreases as a percentage of maximum isometric contraction. And as the velocity of contraction increases during an eccentric contraction (shown by a negative velocity in Figure 2.2b), the force-producing capability of the muscle fibers also increases.

Based upon what has been discussed about activation dynamics, the following point should make sense: As the angular velocity of a movement increases, the joint angle at which maximum force production occurs also increases. In other words, the greater the angular velocity, the farther from initial muscular contraction that the maximum moment about the joint occurs. This is supported by the results found by Bobbert and van Ingen Schenau (1990) using isokinetic testing as well as the data of Gallucci and Challis (2002).

Figure 2.2b is truly a scientific description – albeit a more complicated description – of what's seen in everyday training. When an athlete attempts a one-repetition maximum (1-RM) lift, the weight moves at a very slow velocity during the concentric phase. The slower velocity is a function of the increased load (weight) and, thus, the increased force needed to lift the load.

Figure 2.2b also shows that an athlete can generate more force during the eccentric phase of a lift than during the concentric phase. This is due to a combination of the dynamics of the cross-bridging that occurs between the actin and myosin filaments along with a defense mechanism that the body uses to keep the joint from hyperextending or dislocating. This defense mechanism also relies upon the activation of stabilizing and antagonistic muscles around the joint. The use of eccentric (or negative) training has been used for many years and it's based upon the fact that an athlete can produce more force during this type of motion. This method does have its place in the training of athletes since it can be extremely beneficial for the improvement of force-producing capabilities. But understand that as the load on the muscle is increased, so is the stress on the affiliated joint. Even though greater forces can be produced at greater velocities during eccentric training, it isn't recommended that athletes train eccentrically at high velocities because the risks outweigh the rewards when you consider joint structure and stability. Typically, eccentric training – even with high loads – is performed in a controlled manner. The most common protocols use a count of about 6 - 10 seconds per repetition for the full range of eccentric motion. It's also important that the athlete attempts to keep the velocity of the eccentric contraction constant throughout the range of motion to protect the integrity of the joint.

When training an athlete, it makes sense to perform exercises in the weight room that will have the greatest transfer to the athletic arena. The Law of Specificity suggests that in order for there to be a direct transfer of any exercise to a specific athletic task, the exercise must be *identical* to that task. There's literally no way that anyone can completely mimic a game situation during training and, consequently, no exercise will have a direct transfer to greater performance during any athletic activity. The focus of training should be to enhance *all* aspects of athleticism, knowing that those skills will transfer *only* through the practice of sport-specific skills in whatever the arena may be.

Nowadays, one of the more popular goals of strength-training programs is to develop an athlete's ability to generate power. Since power is a function of force (which is a function of acceleration) and acceleration is a function of the change in velocity, the force-velocity curve of a muscle plays a large role in power development. There are two ways to increase an athlete's ability to produce power: The first is to increase her force-producing capabilities and the second is to increase her rate of force development.

Recall that the formula for power is "force times distance divided by time." A simple way to evaluate power is to consider two athletes – Athlete A and Athlete B, if you will – who have the exact physical structure and perform a barbell squat through an identical range of motion (assumed to be a displacement of the bar a distance of two feet). Now, vary the parameters of force and time. In the first example (focusing solely on the concentric phase of the lift), say that Athlete A can squat 200 pounds in one second and Athlete B can squat 100 pounds in one second. Using the equation for power, Athlete A would have a power output of 400 ft-lb/sec [200 lb x 2 ft ÷ 1.0 sec] and Athlete B would have a power output of 200 ft-lb/sec [100 lb x 2 ft ÷ 1.0 sec]. So Athlete A would be more powerful than Athlete B because she can produce a greater force over the same distance within the same time. In the second example (again focusing solely on the concentric phase), say that Athlete A can squat 100 pounds in 0.5 second and Athlete B can still squat 100 pounds in one second. Using the equation for power, Athlete A would have a power output of 400 ft-lb/sec [100 lb x 2 ft ÷ 0.5 sec] and Athlete B would have a power output of 200 ft-lb/sec [100 lb x 2 ft ÷ 1.0 sec]. Again, Athlete A would be more powerful than Athlete B. As this applies to the force-velocity curve of muscle fibers, both athletes moved the bar at the same velocity in the first example. This is because it took them the same time (one second) to move the bar the same distance (two feet). Therefore, Athlete A produced greater force during a muscular contraction at the same velocity as Athlete B. Both athletes produced the same force (100 pounds) in the second example. Figure 2.2b illustrates that as the velocity of contraction *increases*, the force-producing capability of a muscle *decreases*. This means that if Athlete A can produce the same force at a greater velocity than Athlete B, Athlete A is working at a lower percentage of her maximum isometric contraction. In other words, Athlete A has greater force-producing capabilities than Athlete B in both of the aforementioned examples.

How does this apply to training a female athlete? The answer is quite simple: Just like anything else, the key is the effort that an athlete puts forth. In reality, a comprehensive program should contain exercise of varying velocities. If an athlete is being properly trained, high-velocity exercises don't have to take place in the weight room for an athlete to become more powerful. Power development will occur with proper training at slower velocities if the intensity of the training is at a high level so that the potential for force development will be increased. As demonstrated in both of the previous examples, as an athlete's ability to produce force increases, her ability to produce power also increases.

With that being said, training at higher velocities – that is, using exercises that focus on the rate of force development – can be saved for track workouts and sport-specific, speed-development drills. That is not to say that exercises of higher velocities – such as the Olympic lifts and their variants, box jumps and step-ups – don't have a place in training athletes. The use of these exercises can be traced back a long way and they've been proven to be a successful means of training athletes. Safety does become a factor with these lifts, however, as the increased velocity of the movement can lead to an increased stress on the joint infrastructure. An athlete should only perform such exercises under the strict guidance and supervision of a trained professional.

One last note on power: A true test of power *cannot* include deceleration. The most common test of power is a vertical jump. There's no deceleration during the active phase of a vertical jump. An athlete simply applies as much force to the ground as she can to push herself as high as she can. Any exercise that incorporates a weight that must be caught or stopped at some point in the movement cannot be, by definition, a true test of power. To stop a weight, deceleration must occur at some point. A seated medicine-ball throw would be an accurate measure of upper-body pressing power.

The force-velocity properties of a muscle are also evident in the common training practices known as "plyometrics." During plyometric exercises, an eccentric muscle action – or countermovement – is quickly followed by its reverse concentric action. This is referred to as the "stretch-shortening cycle" (SSC) of a muscle. What occurs initially is that a force is placed upon the active muscle-tendon complex as it lengthens during the eccentric phase of an exercise. This serves to "prime" the muscle for two reasons: First, it allows more time for muscle activation prior to the concentric motion; second, as seen earlier, this is advantageous because a muscle can produce greater force during eccentric motion. In addition, it also provides greater force-producing capabilities because it allows for increased storage of potential energy due to the elastic properties of the muscle-tendon complex. The greater the force that's applied to the structure, the greater the amount of stored energy that will result. In the human body, tendons have a greater potential to stretch prior to the occurrence of damage and, as a result, will be a greater source of stored energy. Figure 2.2c illustrates the tendon force-length curve as a percentage of tendon resting length as it relates to the percentage of maximum isometric force applied to the tendon. Usually, a tendon will lengthen by 4% of its resting length under maximum isometric contraction (Morgan, Proske and Warren 1978; Woittiez et al. 1984; Bobbert et al. 1986). The potential energy that's stored will then be released during the subsequent transition to the concentric motion.

For these reasons, a greater force will be produced during the concentric phase of the movement. Even though plyometric exercises are "quick" in nature, the movements still take place in a favorable position of the force-length curve during the concentric phase. There's an instant during the SSC when the transition from eccentric action changes to concentric action – from stretching to shortening – where the velocity *must* be at zero. In the very beginning stages of the concentric action, then, the muscle is producing forces at or close to that of maximum isometric contractions (Zatsiorsky 1995). Having said that, it has been shown that performing a countermovement prior to a jump will produce a greater performance than not performing a countermovement prior to a jump (Bobbert et al. 1996). This occurs for all of the reasons that have just been discussed.

In essence, every movement in the athletic arena relies on the SSC of muscle to generate force. The wind-up of a softball pitcher is a classic example. Naturally, plyometric exercises that utilize the SSC have become more popular in the training of athletes. Nevertheless, plyometric activities do carry a certain degree of risk and can increase the chance of injury. As stated previously, the success of plyometric exercises relies in part on an increased force placed upon the muscle-tendon complex during the eccentric action. Any force that's placed upon the muscle-tendon complex will also be transferred to the bone structure at the point of the tendon insertion. As many plyometric exercises involve movements of many muscles across many joints, there's a large amount of extra stress placed upon the skeletal system. Because of this, it's recommended that athletes only use plyometric exercises that don't involve high-impact forces and perform a moderate number of ground contacts. Low-level plyometrics – such as jumping rope or doing various skipping exercises – can provide a safe alternative and a productive modality of training. Prior to beginning any jumping exercise, an athlete should also be taught the proper landing position. Failure to land in the proper position will increase the stress on the lower extremities. An athlete must be taught to land softly with her hips back so that her weight isn't over her toes. Figure 2.3 illustrates the proper landing position during a box jump. (Notice the even distribution of the athlete's bodyweight.)

## FINAL THOUGHTS

An understanding of biomechanics is an invaluable tool for a coach or athlete. It becomes far more complicated than what has been discussed in this chapter. Biomechanics helps to promote an understanding of the pathology of injury and, therefore, the proper methods of rehabilitation and prevention. In addition, it can teach proper gait analysis so that an athlete can improve her efficiency when running. Today, computer simulations

**FIGURE 2.3: PROPER LANDING POSITION**
**(Photo by Jason Gallucci)**

can be developed and performed that can teach an athlete how to optimize her performance by altering parameters – such as the angle of release when putting a shot – by simply touching a button. Athletics is one of the biggest businesses – if not *the* biggest business – in our society. It's also a source of entertainment and enjoyment. For these purposes, new research is constantly being conducted to help understand how the body performs. So coaches should continuously review their programs to make sure that they're on the cutting edge. Much of what's known about sport biomechanics today can be obsolete within the next decade. That's why it's important to not only stay on top of the research but also to understand the history of sport and strength training. There are certain principles that have stood the test of time and still hold true to this day. The principles presented in this chapter and book can help mold a productive and efficient philosophy of strength training.

## REFERENCES

Bobbert, M. F., C. Brand, A. de Hann, P. A. Huijing, G. J. van Ingen Schenau, W. H. Rijnsburger and R. D. Woittiez. 1986. Series elasticity of tendinous structures of the rat EDL. *Journal of Physiology* 377: 89P.

Bobbert, M. F., and G. J. van Ingen Schenau. 1990. Isokinetic plantar flexion: experimental results and model calculations. *Journal of Biomechanics* 23 (2): 105-119.

Bobbert, M. F., K. G. M. Gerritsen, M. C. A. Litjens and A. J. van Soest. 1996.

Why is countermovement jump height greater than squat jump height? *Medicine and Science in Sports and Exercise* 28 (11): 1402-1412.

Challis, J. H. 1999. *MuscleLAB manual*. University Park, PA: The Pennsylvania State University.

Fitzhugh, R. 1977. A model of optimal voluntary muscular control. *Journal of Mathematical Biology* 4 (3): 203-236.

Gallucci, J. G., and J. H. Challis. 2002. Examining the role of the gastrocnemius during the leg curl exercise. *Journal of Applied Biomechanics* 18 (1): 15-27.

Henneman, E. 1957. Relation between size of neurons and their susceptibility to discharge. *Science* 126 (3287): 1345-1347.

Hill, A. V. 1938. The heat of shortening and dynamic constants of muscle. *Proceedings of the Royal Society* B126: 136-195.

Huxley, A. F. 1957. Muscle structure and theories of contraction. *Progress in Biophysics and Biophysical Chemistry* 7: 255-318.

Kulig, K., J. G. Andrews and J. G. Hay. 1984. Human strength curves. In *Exercise and sports science reviews* 12, ed. R. L. Terjung, 417-466. New York, NY: McMillan Publishing.

Luther, P. 2003. 3D structure of the sarcomere. Available at *www.sarcomere.org*. Imperial College, London.

Morgan, D. L., U. Proske and D. Warren. 1978. Measurement of muscle stiffness and the mechanism of elastic storage in hopping kangaroos. *Journal of Physiology* 282: 253-261.

Pandy, M. G., F. C. Anderson and D. G. Hull. 1992. A parameter optimization approach for the optimal control of large-scale musculoskeletal systems. *Journal of Biomechanical Engineering* 114 (4): 450-460.

Stein, R., E. P. Zehr and J. Bobet. 2000. Basic concepts of movement control. In *Biomechanics and biology of movement*, ed. B. M. Nigg, B. R. MacIntosh and J. Mester, 163-178. Champaign, IL: Human Kinetics Publishing, Inc.

Woittiez, R. D., P. A. Huijing, H. B. K. Boom and R. H. Rozendal. 1984. A three-dimensional muscle model: a quantified relation between form and function of skeletal muscle. *Journal of Morphology* 182 (1): 95-113.

Zatsiorsky, V. M. 1995. *Science and practice of strength training*. Champaign, IL: Human Kinetics Publishing, Inc.

# 3

# Individualizing Your Workout

*Sam Knopik, M.Ed.*

As strength training becomes more and more a part of an athlete's regimen for success, it's important that she doesn't get lost in the myriad uniformness of training programs. While many athletes may be a part of a team strength and conditioning program, the uniqueness of each athlete should be taken into account.

Athletes who have the ability to develop their own training routine should follow guidelines that take into account several issues and concepts: using the Overload Principle; understanding high volume (many sets) versus high intensity (few sets); recording the progress of strength growth; adding or subtracting sets, intensity builders, days of recovery and exercises; training with an injury; incorporating off-season, in-season and pre-season programs; and developing sport-specific skills.

Assuming that an athlete becomes adept at reading and understanding her workout card and listening to her body, she should be able to continually make the needed adjustments to her workout. These occasional adjustments will lead to more productive and efficient training that will help to prevent injury and enhance athletic performance.

## THE OVERLOAD PRINCIPLE

In order for muscles to become stronger, they must be challenged with a previously unfelt level of stress. This is similar to the process of someone who trains for a marathon, where she would gradually increase her running distances until she was able to perform at the desired level for the desired distance. But rather than training in the weight room to run 26.2 miles, the goal is to simply make her a stronger athlete through resistance training. From workout to workout, an athlete must do one of two things to apply the Overload Principle: Add more resistance or add more repetitions.

This concept is easily put into practice. As an athlete continues through her workout and keeps good records of her progress, she should force herself to perform one or more repetitions (with the same resistance) than she did in her previous workout. This application is exemplified in Figure 3.1. Once an athlete has reached the top of her prescribed repetition range (both examples use a range of 15 - 20), she should increase the resistance. This application is exemplified in Figure 3.2. These are both examples of the Overload Principle in

| EXERCISES | REP RANGE | DEC 1 weight / reps | DEC 3 weight / reps | DEC 5 weight / reps | DEC 8 weight / reps |
|-----------|-----------|------|------|------|------|
| Leg Press | 15-20 | 145 / 15 | 145 / 17 | 145 / 19 | 145 / 21 |

**FIGURE 3.1: THE OVERLOAD PRINCIPLE – INCREASING REPETITIONS**

| EXERCISES | REP RANGE | DEC 10 weight / reps | DEC 12 weight / reps | DEC 15 weight / reps | DEC 17 weight / reps |
|-----------|-----------|------|------|------|------|
| Leg Press | 15-20 | 145 / 21 | 155 / 18 | 155 / 20 | 165 / 16 |

**FIGURE 3.2: THE OVERLOAD PRINCIPLE – INCREASING RESISTANCE**

action. You can rest assured that if one or both of these key requirements (resistance and repetitions) are going up, an athlete's muscles are getting stronger.

## VOLUME VERSUS INTENSITY

All workouts involve a critical relationship between volume and intensity. Essentially, volume refers to the amount of time that's spent doing physical training. Every set or exercise that's added to a routine increases the volume of the workout. "Intensity" refers to the level of effort that an athlete demonstrates during her physical training. It's important to understand that volume and intensity are on opposite ends of the training spectrum. Think about it: If the volume (duration) of training is high, the intensity of training is low. Since it's desired that the level of intensity is high, the volume of training must be low. Performing a minimal number of sets and exercises to the point of momentary muscular fatigue (MMF) represents a protocol characterized by a high level of intensity.

Basing the development of strength on the Overload Principle – as explained previously – ways must be found to produce an "overload." Essentially, this can be done through high volume or high intensity. Depending upon where an athlete is in her development, both modes can be used. It should be noted, however, that if an athlete demonstrates the ability to train with a high level of intensity, she should begin to reduce the volume of her workout.

High-volume protocols can be used when an athlete begins a strength-training program. As the main objective is to produce an "overload," an athlete who's new to the weight room – that is, a novice lifter – may need the additional volume to fully fatigue her muscles. In order to exhaust a muscle to the point of fatigue, an athlete must be strong of mind. Although this can be developed, it would be unrealistic to assume that a novice lifter understands the concept of MMF. Thus, a higher volume of training could make up for a lower level of intensity.

From workout to workout, an athlete must do one of two things to apply the Overload Principle: Add more resistance or add more repetitions. (Photo by Pete Silletti)

In addition to giving the working muscles more sets to produce fatigue, a novice lifter will develop the neuromuscular pathways for each unique exercise. Once an athlete has mastered these exercises while demonstrating proper form and repetition speed, she can focus more on producing a desirable level of intensity.

## THE IMPORTANCE OF RECORD KEEPING

Too many athletes approach their strength training without an understanding of progression. If an athlete is making her way around the weight room without recording her performance on a workout card or in a notebook, it can be assumed that she isn't interested in developing strength effectively. Remember that the objective is to gradually produce an "overload." Using a workout card can simplify the process of knowing when to increase the resistance as well as quantify improvements in strength.

When maintaining a proper record of strength training, it's important to keep an accurate track of the vital information such as the date of the workout and the resistance used on the set to MMF along with the number of repetitions completed with good technique. If an athlete is using a high-volume approach, she should make a note of how many sets she performs but should record only the repetitions of her first set since that's the first one taken to MMF.

It's desired that the first set be taken to MMF. The sets that follow should be decreased in weight but also taken to MMF. This ensures that an accurate measurement of strength growth is obtained before an athlete is exhausted from doing multiple sets (which makes it difficult to quantify the effort). Again, as an athlete becomes more comfortable with an exercise and shows the capacity to consistently demonstrate high levels of intensity, her volume – in terms of sets – should be reduced.

Before beginning an exercise, an athlete should review her workout card to determine how much resistance to use. If the resistance used in the previous workout was too light and she finished above the prescribed repetition range, she should increase the weight. An increase in the resistance of 5% should be adequate but an athlete should consult with her coach or use her best judgment in this regard to ensure that the weight offers a challenge. If the resistance used in the previous workout was too heavy and she finished below the prescribed repetition range, she should decrease the weight. If the resistance used in the previous workout was just right and she finished within the prescribed repetition range, she should use the same weight and strive for at least one more repetition.

At the completion of the set she – or her training partner – should record the number of repetitions that were successfully completed with good technique and note the resistance for her next workout. This step saves time in the subsequent workout in that the only thing the athlete has to do when approaching the exercise is to note the pre-recorded resistance and begin her set.

When using machines with weight stacks, it's beneficial to simply count the number of plates to be lifted as opposed to using the numbers that are printed on the plates. Some strength coaches have gone as far as removing the painted numbers on the plates and replacing them with letters. This can save time and prevent confusion when you come across machines that have several sets of numbers. Finally, this also makes lifting weights less intimidating and competitive. Indeed, those who have a low potential for increasing strength can become discouraged and frustrated when discussions of training invariably shift to comparisons of lifting prowess with the ubiquitous question of "How much can you bench press?" Clearly, an athlete will be less intimidated by this question if she can respond with a letter rather than a number.

The bottom line is that without an accurate record of what an athlete has previously done, it becomes impossible to efficiently overload her muscles. In addition, tracking the development of strength becomes a guessing game and training sessions could become dangerous as athletes use amounts of resistance for which they may not be physically prepared. On the other hand, using a well-designed workout card is not only safe but can serve as a terrific motivator for an athlete as she begins to see improvements in strength and meet training goals.

Athletes can benefit from using higher repetition ranges just as they would from using lower repetition ranges. (Photo by Pete Silletti)

## TROUBLESHOOTING THE WORKOUT

Once an athlete has begun her training using the concepts that were outlined earlier, there will come a time to make modifications to her workout. This is what's called "individualizing the workout." Athletes aren't clones of each other. Thus, their training should be approached as unique and modifications should be made as necessary. The following can be used as a guide for adding or subtracting sets, repetitions (in a repetition range), intensity builders, days of recovery and/or exercises.

### Sets

As mentioned earlier, the use of multiple sets should be employed with novice lifters (or even some intermediate ones). Higher volume can be substituted for higher intensity but remember, there's a tradeoff. Obviously, multiple sets will take more time to complete and athletes shouldn't expect to train productively for much more than 60 minutes at a time.

Assuming that an athlete uses three sets, records her performance on the first set and begins to demonstrate higher levels of intensity, she should reduce her sets from three to two. If after a week or two, her levels of strength continue to increase and her intensity and lifting technique remain solid, she should reduce her sets from two to one.

Multiple sets may be prescribed for an athlete who struggles with learning proper technique or demonstrates undesirable levels of intensity. Recall that "overload" must be produced to develop strength. Until overload can be done with high intensity, it should be done with high volume.

### Repetition Ranges

Depending upon the body part being worked, standard repetition ranges can be used when developing a training protocol. These ranges would be 15 - 20 for exercises employing the hips and major lower-body, multiple-joint movements such as the leg press and trap-bar deadlift; 10 - 15 for lower-body, single-joint movements such as the leg extension and leg curl; 8 - 12 for upper-body, multiple-joint movements such as the chest press or lat pulldown; and 6 - 12 for upper-body, single-joint movements such as the bicep curl and tricep extension.

The reason that higher repetition ranges are used in the lower-body movements – especially the multiple-joint movements – is due to safety. If the repetition ranges are increased, the resistance must be decreased which will generally make the exercise safer. Remember, gains in strength aren't resigned to certain repetition ranges. So athletes can benefit from using higher repetition ranges just as they would from using lower repetition ranges. As long as an athlete improves upon the number of repetitions that she did relative to a previous workout, she'll produce an overload. The advantage of using a higher repetition range, though, is safety. Because one of the primary purposes of training is to reduce/avoid injury on the athletic fields, it's irresponsible and nonsensical to sustain an injury while training in the weight room.

Now, there may come a time when an athlete discovers that she may have to increase or decrease a repetition range. If an athlete continually struggles to advance beyond a particular repetition, she could reduce the repetition range to coincide with that number. For instance, if it was impossible for an athlete to do more than 10 repetitions in an exercise for several workouts – and assuming that she demonstrated a high level of intensity – it's reasonable to conclude that she carries a higher percentage of fast-twitch (FT) muscle fibers than the average person. These FT fibers fatigue quickly and would, thus, hamper her ability to perform with high levels of intensity beyond a certain number of repetitions. An adjustment can be made to the repetition range by lowering it from 8 - 12 to 6 - 10, for example.

Finally, repetition ranges may need to be modified to suit the needs of adolescent or novice lifters. This is done by increasing the repetition range which will require an athlete to lighten the resistance. Again, the resistance is reduced to protect young athletes' bodies as well as to train their neuromuscular pathways for each exercise.

## Days of Recovery

Every strength-training athlete will occasionally reach what's called a "plateau" of strength gains. This means that the athlete is struggling to get beyond a certain number of repetitions with a certain level of resistance. There are numerous reasons why plateaus could happen. When attempting to troubleshoot this problem, things to be considered include overtraining, poor sleeping habits, nutritional needs or levels of intensity.

A fact that many athletes disregard is that sometimes recovery is the best medicine. If an athlete is stuck on the eighth repetition on a chest press and her level of intensity is high, she could either skip that movement for a workout or take off an additional day from training. Many times, taking off this extra day will allow her body enough recovery and lead to additional gains in strength.

This fact contradicts the common perception of "more is better." Training with a high level of intensity isn't easy. An athlete will need time to recover as will her mind. Don't underestimate the benefits that one can derive from an additional day away from training. Chances are that an athlete's body could use the recovery and her hunger to return to training could lead to higher levels of intensity.

Overtraining occurs when the muscles aren't given adequate recovery between workout days. The body typically needs 2 - 3 days to fully recover from a strength-training workout. But depending upon an athlete's level of intensity, she may need just 48 hours . . . or she could need up to one entire week! Here's the bottom line on recovery: When an athlete reaches a strength plateau and her level of intensity is high, she should be given additional recovery. Her body will reward and thank her.

## Intensity Builders

Another way to break through a training plateau is to increase the intensity of the set taken to MMF. An athlete needs to use caution when employing an intensity builder as the risk of overtraining is greater. If used sparingly, however, an intensity builder can be just what's needed to "overload" the muscles enough to trigger a growth spurt.

Building up the intensity output is relatively simple and an athlete has a variety of options from which to choose. Following a set to MMF, an athlete's partner could help her perform breakdowns, negatives, static holds or manual resistance. Each of these types of intensity builders should occur immediately following the last repetition of a set taken to MMF. The additional work required by the muscle may be enough to create sufficient "overload."

When performing intensity builders, the use of a training partner is highly recommended (and required for use with free weights). Manual resistance is a super alternative to traditional resistance exercises. The partner simply mimics the exercise with the use of her hands. (Manual-resistance exercises are discussed in great detail in Chapter 5.) Regardless of the type of intensity-building technique used, an athlete should do them sparingly and be aware of the possibility of overtraining.

## Dealing with an Injury

Injury is a fact of life in sports that most athletes will have to face at one time or another. However, many injuries will not prohibit an athlete from strength training altogether. In fact, strength training may be an excellent way to begin the recovery process.

If an injury is isolated to one particular body part – such as the left arm or leg – an athlete can train "around" that body part. An athlete can do this by incorporating exercises that don't involve the injured limb. Likewise, an athlete can begin to use relatively light amounts of resistance in order to bring an injured body part back to full strength. It's highly recommended that an injured athlete seek medical attention before attempting to rehabilitate an injury. (For more information on rehabilitative training, refer to Chapter 8.)

## Off-Season, Pre-Season and In-Season Training

If an athlete truly believes that strength training is beneficial for her development as an athlete, she should make a commitment to train throughout the entire year. Traditionally, many have bought into the belief that athletes "bulk" in the off-season, "tone" in the pre-season and "maintain" during the season. But the reality is this: For an athlete to realize her physical potential, she must develop her strength throughout the entire year. Is an athlete lifting more resistance or performing more repetitions? If so, who cares what time of year it is? She's making great strides to become a better athlete.

The only modification one should make during the season would be the amount of recovery time allotted before the next contest. Performing workouts of high-intensity the day of or the day before a game should be discouraged due to insufficient recovery. Remember that a large part of high-intensity training is to increase the level of performance on game day. Honor the fact that an athlete trains hard and her body needs adequate time to recover.

## Sport-Specific Skill Work

The ultimate way to individualize a workout would be for athletes to incorporate drill work that they'll actually use while competing. This doesn't mean having them jump off a plyometric box with a pair of dumbbells just because they jump to block or spike a volleyball! What it does mean is that after completing a workout – assuming that they have the energy – they can go down to the gymnasium and get on the volleyball court. Here, the athletes can run through a series of blocking and hitting drills that will require them to jump near the net.

It's obvious to those athletes who strength train that their sport-specific skills can be enhanced but it should be understood that those sport-specific skills must be practiced. If an athlete desires to improve her skill at blocking, for example, then she must practice blocking. However, an athlete who develops power in her lower body in the weight room by strengthening her hips and legs and practices blocking on the volleyball court should greatly improve her skills.

Understand that there are no movements that are done in the weight room that should or can simulate sport-specific skills. It should be an athlete's intention to improve her strength and power in the weight room and then to develop the skills necessary for her sport in the appropriate athletic arena.

## CONCLUSION

While talent levels will vary from athlete to athlete, strength training gives all athletes the opportunity to improve themselves. With this improvement, one can hope to become a better competitor in her sport of choice. Recognizing that not all athletes are the same, it should be no surprise that various considerations should be made depending upon each athlete. By taking the proper steps and correctly reading the signs, an athlete can create a safe and productive strength-training regimen.

# 4

# Intensity-Building Techniques

*Sam Knopik, M.Ed.*

Due to the fact that muscles adapt and grow in response to a progressive increase in resistance and/or repetitions – also known as the Overload Principle – it's important for athletes to work as hard as they possibly can. The ability to push oneself during a workout is called "intensity." Understand that intensity isn't the ability to groan and moan really loud or move the resistance at high speeds. Rather, intensity should be understood as the ability to work the muscles to the point of momentary muscular fatigue (MMF). When needed, there are certain techniques that will allow athletes to increase their levels of intensity.

There will come a time in the training process where an athlete becomes "stuck" or reaches a "plateau" at a particular resistance or repetition. As noted in Chapter 3, there are a variety of ways to overcome this, one being intensity builders. An intensity builder is an activity or method that's introduced to the training regimen briefly and infrequently to stimulate muscular growth through additional overload.

It should be understood that intensity builders – if used too often or incorrectly – could lead to overtraining and injury. The person who is working with an athlete as her spotter – either a coach, trainer or another athlete – should be

**Intensity should be understood as the ability to work the muscles to the point of momentary muscular fatigue. (Photo by Pete Silletti)**

just as familiar with the technique and administration of the intensity builders as the athlete herself. When used judiciously, however, intensity builders can be the perfect jump-start for muscular growth and productive training.

## TYPES OF INTENSITY BUILDERS

There are a number of intensity builders. The most popular ones include negatives, forced repetitions, breakdowns, 30s and manual resistance.

### Negatives

A repetition has two phases: concentric (or positive) and eccentric (or negative). Simply, the concentric phase is when the weight is being raised; the eccentric phase is when the weight is being lowered. In the leg press, for example, the concentric phase is when the lifter pushes the foot pedal away from her body (by extending her hips and legs); the eccentric phase is when she returns the foot pedal toward her body.

It has been scientifically established that a fresh, un-fatigued muscle can produce about 40% more force during the eccentric phase of a repetition in comparison to the concentric phase of a repetition. Therefore, an athlete will *always* reach MMF during the concentric phase of the repetition. But because a muscle can produce force in both the concentric and eccentric phases, it should be worked during both phases. The proper use of negatives allows an athlete to fully exhaust her working muscle(s) during the eccentric phase well after fatigue or "failure" has been reached during the concentric phase.

Negatives are done *immediately* after a lifter reaches MMF. To perform a negative, a coach or training partner raises the resistance to the fully contracted position (which is also referred to as the "mid-range" or "mid-point" position). Then, the lifter lowers the resistance in a very slow and controlled manner. A negative should take about 6 - 8 seconds with the spotter counting cadence out loud to ensure a proper speed. Depending upon the desired level of intensity, one or two negatives can be administered at the end of a set (after the lifter attains MMF).

To illustrate, assume that a lifter reached MMF on the leg press during her 16th repetition. (In other words, she tried to do the 16th repetition but was unable to complete it.) Her training partner immediately helps the lifter raise the weight to the fully contracted position where her hips and legs are extended. At this point, the lifter begins to lower the resistance slowly as her spotter counts "Eight . . . seven . . . six . . . five . . . four . . . three . . . two . . . one . . . stretch." Sometimes, the lifter is still quite strong in the eccentric phase even after reaching MMF. In this case, the spotter may need to add some of her bodyweight to the resistance to fully challenge and fatigue the lifter's eccentric strength (assuming that it's safe to do so). In a bench press with a barbell, for example, the training partner should be more concerned with spotting the lifter for safety than with applying extra resistance to the bar. For this reason, it's strongly encouraged that machine exercises are used instead of free-weight exercises when administering negatives.

Since this intensity builder could – if used incorrectly – compromise the safety of the lifter, the spotter should be schooled in the finer points of doling out negatives.

## Forced Repetitions

At the end of every "work set" to fatigue, a lifter will come to the point where she's no longer able to perform the concentric phase of the repetition. The lifter can still generate concentric force but not enough to lift the weight. In order to fatigue greater amounts of muscle fibers, the lifter – with assistance from her spotter – can perform what are called "forced repetitions."

A forced repetition is administered immediately after the lifter reaches MMF. At this point, the spotter encourages the lifter to lower the weight slowly and in control. (Remember, the lifter is always stronger during the eccentric phase even after reaching MMF.) The spotter then assists the lifter in performing the concentric phase of the repetition. The assistance from the spotter should be very minimal – just enough to help the lifter raise the weight. Depending upon the desired level of intensity, one or two forced repetitions can be administered at the end of a set (after the lifter attains MMF).

Again, safety should be stressed when using forced repetitions. Machine exercises provide an excellent means by which to execute forced repetitions in a safe manner. If done with a free-weight exercise – such as a bench press with a barbell – the spotter should be in a stable position and physically capable of fully assisting the lifter when needed.

## Breakdowns

Breakdowns follow the same procedure as the forced repetitions and should begin following the point of MMF. Once an athlete reaches MMF, she should "rack" the weight (or return it to the starting position). Then, the athlete and/or her spotter should reduce the resistance and immediately perform the exercise to MMF again – this time with the lighter load.

Keep in mind that the role of the spotter is just as important during breakdowns as it is during negatives or forced repetitions since the lifter's form might deteriorate as she becomes more and more fatigued and safety may be compromised. This can be repeated for one additional set or as many as desired. However, the lifter should be reminded that overtraining is a risk with any intensity builder – especially from the use of breakdowns.

## 30s

The use of 30-repetition sets – or "30s" – should be preplanned and added to the workout with the understanding that it isn't a "conventional" routine. When doing 30s, the lifter may choose to complete her usual routine of exercises or limit it to as few as six – just enough exercises to address every muscle in her body either directly or indirectly.

The lifter should use a resistance that's at or lower than her normal workload for a given exercise. She would complete no less than 30 repetitions

When doing 30s, the lifter should use a resistance that's at or lower than her normal workload for a given exercise. (Photo by Pete Silletti)

of that exercise before moving to the next one. Again, this isn't a standard workout format and differs significantly from other intensity builders in that 30s cannot simply be done at the end of a typical "work set" after reaching MMF.

If desired, an athlete can increase her "30s Day" to 40s, 50s or more. And with a little ingenuity, these intensity builders can be made into an event that's really exciting. Coach Mike Lawrence, the head strength and conditioning coach at Missouri Southern University, plays 80s music that blasts over the facility's speakers to signify the arrival of 80s Day to his athletes!

## Manual Resistance

Probably the most efficient and safest way to add intensity to a workout is to include manual-resistance exercises. Manual resistance is simply the use of a training partner as the resistance for the exercise. Typically, the training partners use their hands to essentially mimic a conventional exercise.

Similar to the use of negatives, forced repetitions and breakdowns, manual resistance can be used as a type of "finisher" to an exercise. Or, manual resistance can be performed as a separate movement itself. As an example of how manual resistance would be incorporated at the end of a set, suppose that a lifter reached MMF in the shoulder press with dumbbells. At this point, the lifter should put the dumbbells on the floor. Then, the spotter would position herself so that she can grasp hands with the lifter and apply downward force on her hands. The lifter should push against the spotter's hands in the same manner as if she was doing the shoulder press with dumbbells. The spotter should apply enough force to make the lifter work but should understand that the lifter is already quite fatigued, having just done the exercise to MMF. Therefore, the spotter should adjust the amount of resistance so that it's appropriate to the lifter's level of fatigue.

Regardless of its use as an intensity builder, manual resistance is a tremendously efficient and extremely safe way to train. Keep in mind, though, that one drawback of manual resistance is that the resistance cannot be quantified thereby making it literally impossible to measure gains in strength and resistance. (For more information on manual-resistance exercises, refer to Chapter 5.)

## CLOSING THOUGHTS

It's known that once muscles are progressively challenged to adapt to increased stress – through either more resistance or repetitions – they grow. Once it has been fully exhausted, placing any further demands upon a muscle increases the amount of time that it will need to recover. Therefore, intensity builders should be used carefully. An athlete should know why she's adding an intensity builder to her workout and the training partner or spotter should be educated beforehand. Remember, intensity builders are sound ways to add variety to a workout and may help an athlete overcome the dreaded strength plateau.

# 5

# Manual Resistance: Strength Training Without Weights

*Scott Savor, B.S.*

Manual Resistance (MR) is a productive form of strength training without weights. Unlike most traditional methods, MR can be implemented into any strength-training program. With MR, a partner or spotter supplies resistance to stimulate proper overload of the musculature.

Muscles don't have eyeballs and could care less about the source of resistance. Therefore, MR – when performed properly – can produce favorable results. In order to reap the best response from MR, the muscle(s) should be worked to muscular fatigue or "failure" (when no further repetitions can be completed with proper technique) within appropriate ranges of time: about 60 - 90 seconds for the lower body and 40 - 70 seconds for the upper body. Also, all repetitions should be performed with the following cadence: at least a two-second concentric (raising) phase, a brief pause in the contracted (or mid-point) position and at least a four-second eccentric (lowering) phase. This speed of movement will minimize the involvement of momentum.

It's important to understand that many factors will affect an athlete's results such as her genetics, eating and sleeping habits and level of intensity (or effort). Aside from that, MR is extremely efficient in a setting that has equipment limitations or when training a large number of athletes. In fact, MR has

**With manual resistance, a partner or spotter supplies resistance to stimulate proper overload of the musculature. (Photo by Scott Savor)**

been used for many years in professional athletics and medical settings and at major universities. It can also provide much variety for workouts to help eliminate staleness and boredom (Haney 1997).

Don't be fooled into thinking that because MR involves little or no equipment, that it's easy. D'Amato (2001) states that "an all manual resistance workout is one of the toughest workouts you can do if you go all-out."

## ADVANTAGES AND DISADVANTAGES

Like all other forms of strength training, MR has advantages as well as disadvantages. What follows are the major advantages and disadvantages of MR.

### Advantages:

- It provides variety for workouts.
- The speed of movement can be controlled.
- A large number of athletes can be trained at once.
- The muscles can be worked maximally during each repetition.
- Equipment usually isn't needed to perform the exercises.
- The exercises can be done virtually anywhere.
- The level of intensity can be controlled (to a certain degree).

### Disadvantages:

- Two people are needed.
- It's impossible to chart progress.
- The lifter must be motivated enough to perform the exercise correctly and exert maximum force throughout the entire repetition.
- The strength levels of the lifter and spotter must be somewhat similar.
- The spotter must be able to apply the resistance safely and effectively.

## RESPONSIBILITIES

With MR, the spotter and lifter have certain responsibilities that must be met in order to produce the maximum possible benefits. What follows are the major responsibilities of the spotter and lifter.

### The Spotter:

- Make sure that each exercise is done in a safe manner.
- Communicate properly with the lifter at all times.
- Give the lifter more resistance during the eccentric phase of each repetition.
- Adjust the resistance based upon changes in the lifter's biomechanical leverage and path of her limb(s).
- Coach proper lifting techniques and relaxed breathing.

One of the major responsibilities of the spotter is to motivate the lifter. (Photo by Scott Savor)

- Motivate the lifter.
- Insist on a full range of motion for each repetition.
- Change from the concentric phase to the eccentric phase in a smooth manner.

## The Lifter:

- Ease into the first few repetitions to warm up the targeted muscles.
- Pause briefly in the contracted position.
- Keep the muscles loaded throughout the entire repetition.
- Communicate properly with the spotter at all times.
- Emphasize the eccentric phase of each repetition.
- Concentrate on using only those muscles that are targeted in the exercise.
- Change from the concentric phase to the eccentric phase in a smooth manner.
- Achieve a full range of motion for each repetition.
- Train with a high level of intensity.

## THE EXERCISES

This chapter will describe the safest and most productive exercises that can be performed with MR. Included in the discussions of each exercise are the muscle(s) worked (if more than one muscle is involved, the first muscle listed is the prime mover); suggested repetitions (the time that the targeted muscles should be loaded is shown in parentheses); brief but specific instructions as to how the spotter and lifter should perform the exercise; and training guidelines for the lifter to make the exercise safer and more productive. (In the subsequent photographs that accompany the exercises, the lifter is wearing a dark top and the spotter is wearing a white top.)

The 26 exercises described in this chapter are posterior neck, lateral neck, anterior neck, posterior raise, lateral raise, anterior raise, diagonal raise, shoulder shrug, upright row, shoulder press, external rotation, internal rotation, chest fly, push-up, low row, bent-over row, tricep extension, bicep curl, incline bicep, back extension, hip abduction, hip adduction, hip flexion, leg curl, leg extension and dorsi flexion.

## POSTERIOR NECK

Start/Finish

Mid-point

**Muscles Worked:** neck extensors and trapezius (upper)

**Suggested Repetitions:** 6 - 12 (or 40 - 70 seconds)

**Spotter:** Kneel in front of the lifter and place your thumbs together on the back of her head, supporting her neck region.

**Lifter:** Kneel in front of the spotter, place your forearms flat on the floor, bend your elbows, relax your shoulders and bring your chin toward your chest. To do the exercise, extend your head backward.

**Training Guideline (lifter):** Keep your elbows on the floor and relax your shoulders as you perform this exercise.

## LATERAL NECK

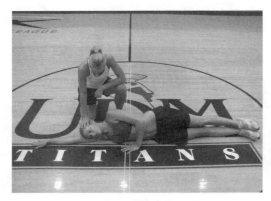

**Start/Finish**

**Mid-point**

**Muscle Worked:** sternocleidomastoideus (one side)

**Suggested Repetitions:** 6 - 12 (or 40 - 70 seconds)

**Spotter:** Kneel behind the lifter, place your right hand flat against the left side of her head with your index (or pointer) finger and thumb around her ear.

**Lifter:** Lie on the floor on your right side in front of the spotter, place your head on your right arm and look straight ahead. To do the exercise, bring your head toward your left shoulder. Repeat the exercise for the other side of your body.

**Training Guideline (lifter):** Relax your shoulders as you perform this exercise.

## ANTERIOR NECK

**Start/Finish**

**Mid-point**

**Muscle Worked:** sternocleidomastoideus (both sides)

**Suggested Repetitions:** 6 - 12 (or 40 - 70 seconds)

**Spotter:** Kneel behind the lifter's head, overlap your hands and place them on her forehead.

**Lifter:** Lie supine on the floor in front of the spotter, externally rotate your arms at about 90 degrees, keep the backs of your arms on the floor, bend your knees and place your feet flat on the floor. To do the exercise, bring your chin toward your chest.

**Training Guideline (lifter):** Keep your shoulders on the floor as you perform this exercise.

## POSTERIOR RAISE

**Start/Finish**

**Mid-point**

**Muscles Worked:** posterior deltoid and trapezius (middle)

**Suggested Repetitions:** 6 - 12 (or 40 - 70 seconds)

**Spotter:** Stand in front of the lifter and place your hands flat against her wrists.

**Lifter:** Sit on a bench, lean against the back pad (if one is available), straighten your arms and position them so that they're perpendicular to your torso. To do the exercise, keep your arms straight and draw them backward as far as possible.

**Training Guideline (lifter):** Sit tall and keep your torso against the back pad (if one is available) as you perform this exercise.

## LATERAL RAISE

**Start/Finish**

**Mid-point**

**Muscles Worked:** middle deltoid and supraspinatus

**Suggested Repetitions:** 6 - 12 (or 40 - 70 seconds)

**Spotter:** Stand behind the lifter and place your hands flat somewhere between her elbows and wrists.

**Lifter:** Stand in front of the spotter, spread your feet apart a comfortable distance and straighten your arms. To do the exercise, keep your arms straight and raise them sideways until they're roughly parallel to the floor.

**Training Guideline (lifter):** Stand tall and relax your back as you perform this exercise.

## ANTERIOR RAISE

**Start/Finish**

**Mid-point**

**Muscle Worked:** anterior deltoid

**Suggested Repetitions:** 6 - 12 (or 40 - 70 seconds)

**Spotter:** Stand in front of the lifter and place your hands flat against her wrists.

**Lifter:** Stand in front of the spotter, spread your feet apart a comfortable distance and straighten your arms. To do the exercise, keep your arms straight and raise them forward until they're roughly parallel to the floor.

**Training Guideline (lifter):** Stand tall and keep your back straight as you perform this exercise.

## DIAGONAL RAISE

Start/Finish

Mid-point

**Muscles Worked:** middle deltoid and anterior deltoid

**Suggested Repetitions:** 6 - 12 (or 40 - 70 seconds)

**Spotter:** Stand near the lifter's right side and place your right hand flat against her right wrist.

**Lifter:** Sit on a bench, lean against the back pad (if one is available), straighten your right arm and place your right hand on your left leg near your knee. To do the exercise, raise your right arm in a diagonal plane until it's roughly parallel to the floor. Repeat the exercise for the other side of your body.

**Training Guideline (lifter):** Sit tall and keep your torso against the back pad (if one is available) as you perform this exercise.

## SHOULDER SHRUG

**Start/Finish**

**Mid-point**

**Muscle Worked:** trapezius (upper)

**Suggested Repetitions:** 6 - 12 (or 40 - 70 seconds)

**Spotter:** Lie supine on the floor between the lifter's feet and grasp the middle of a towel.

**Lifter:** Stand upright, place your feet alongside the spotter's hips, grasp one end of a towel in each hand, tuck your chin and straighten your arms. To do the exercise, raise your shoulders as high as possible.

**Training Guideline (lifter):** Don't round or "roll" your shoulders as you perform this exercise.

## UPRIGHT ROW

**Start/Finish**

**Mid-point**

**Muscles Worked:** anterior deltoid, middle deltoid, trapezius (upper) and bi-ceps

**Suggested Repetitions:** 6 - 12 (or 40 - 70 seconds)

**Spotter:** Kneel in front of the lifter and grasp the middle of a towel.

**Lifter:** Stand in front of the spotter, grasp one end of a towel in each hand, straighten your arms, tuck your chin and spread your feet apart a comfort-able distance. To do the exercise, pull your hands toward your chin while keeping them close to your body.

**Training Guideline (lifter):** Keep your back straight and your elbows high as you perform this exercise.

## SHOULDER PRESS

**Start/Finish**

**Mid-point**

**Muscles Worked:** anterior deltoid, middle deltoid and triceps

**Suggested Repetitions:** 6 - 12 (or 40 - 70 seconds)

**Spotter:** Stand behind the lifter and place your hands on top of her hands.

**Lifter:** Sit on the floor in front of the spotter, lean back against her legs, position your hands near your shoulders and cross your legs. To do the exercise, straighten your arms by pushing against the spotter's hands.

**Training Guideline (lifter):** Sit tall and lower your hands in the eccentric phase to the point where the angle between your upper and lower arms is slightly less than 90 degrees as you perform this exercise.

## EXTERNAL ROTATION

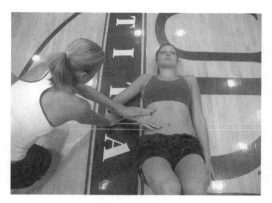

Start/Finish

Mid-point

**Muscles Worked:** external rotators (infraspinatus and teres minor)

**Suggested Repetitions:** 6 - 12 (or 40 - 70 seconds)

**Spotter:** Kneel near the lifter's right side, place your left hand flat against the back of her right wrist and support her right elbow with your right hand.

**Lifter:** Lie supine on the floor near the spotter, bend your right arm so that the angle between your upper and lower arms is about 90 degrees, position your right hand against your mid-section and open your right hand. To do the exercise, push your right hand away from your mid-section while maintaining the same angle between your upper and lower arms. Repeat the exercise for the other side of your body.

**Training Guideline (lifter):** Keep your upper arm stationary as you perform this exercise.

## INTERNAL ROTATION

**Start/Finish**

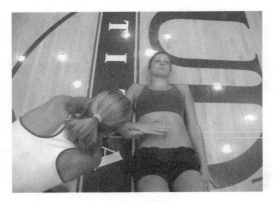

**Mid-point**

**Muscles Worked:** internal rotators (subscapularis and teres major)

**Suggested Repetitions:** 6 - 12 (or 40 - 70 seconds)

**Spotter:** Kneel near the lifter's right side, place your left hand flat against the front of her right wrist and support her right elbow with your right hand.

**Lifter:** Lie supine on the floor near the spotter, bend your right arm so that the angle between your upper and lower arms is about 90 degrees, position your left hand away from your mid-section and open your right hand. To do the exercise, pull your right hand toward your mid-section while maintaining the same angle between your upper and lower arms. Repeat the exercise for the other side of your body.

**Training Guideline (lifter):** Keep your upper arm stationary as you perform this exercise.

## CHEST FLY

Start/Finish

Mid-point

**Muscles Worked:** pectoralis major and anterior deltoid

**Suggested Repetitions:** 6 - 12 (or 40 - 70 seconds)

**Spotter:** Kneel above the lifter's head and place your hands flat against the insides of her elbows.

**Lifter:** Lie supine on the floor in front of the spotter, interlock your fingers behind your head, bend your knees and place your feet flat on the floor. To do the exercise, bring your elbows together.

**Training Guideline (lifter):** Keep your head down and your back flat as you perform this exercise.

## PUSH-UP

**Start/Finish**

**Mid-point**

**Muscles Worked:** pectoralis major, anterior deltoid and triceps

**Suggested Repetitions:** 6 - 12 (or 40 - 70 seconds)

**Spotter:** Position your feet alongside the lifter's hips and place your hands flat on her upper back.

**Lifter:** Lie prone on the floor between the spotter's feet and position your hands just below your shoulders. To do the exercise, straighten your arms by pushing through the heels of your hands while keeping your abdominals tight and back flat.

**Training Guideline (lifter):** Keep your entire body as straight as possible as you perform this exercise.

## LOW ROW

Start/Finish

Mid-point

**Muscles Worked:** latissimus dorsi ("lats"), biceps and forearms

**Suggested Repetitions:** 6 - 12 (or 40 - 70 seconds)

**Spotter:** Sit on the floor in front of the lifter, spread your feet apart, straighten your legs and grasp the middle of a towel.

**Lifter:** Sit on the floor in front of the spotter, place the soles of your feet against the soles of her feet, straighten your legs, torso and arms and grasp one end of a towel in each hand. To do the exercise, pull your hands toward your chest while keeping your elbows close to your torso.

**Training Guideline (lifter):** Sit tall as you perform this exercise.

## BENT-OVER ROW

**Start/Finish**

**Mid-point**

**Muscle Worked:** latissimus dorsi ("lats")

**Suggested Repetitions:** 6 - 12 (or 40 - 70 seconds)

**Spotter:** Stand near the lifter's right side, place your right hand just above her right elbow and your left hand on her upper back.

**Lifter:** Place your left knee and left hand on the back pad of a bench and let your right arm hang straight down. To do the exercise, raise your right arm while keeping your right elbow close to your torso. Repeat the exercise for the other side of your body.

**Training Guideline (lifter):** Keep your torso approximately parallel to the floor as you perform this exercise.

## TRICEP EXTENSION

Start/Finish

Mid-point

**Muscle Worked:** tricep group (the middle, long and lateral heads)

**Suggested Repetitions:** 6 - 12 (or 40 - 70 seconds)

**Spotter:** Position your feet alongside the lifter's chest (while facing her head) and place your hands on her wrists.

**Lifter:** Lie supine on the floor between the spotter's feet, make two fists and put them together above your forehead, place the backs of your upper arms against her lower legs, bend your knees and place your feet flat on the floor. To do the exercise, straighten your arms.

**Training Guideline (lifter):** Relax your shoulders as you perform this exercise.

## BICEP CURL

**Start/Finish**

**Mid-point**

**Muscle Worked:** biceps

**Suggested Repetitions:** 6 - 12 (or 40 - 70 seconds)

**Spotter:** Stand in front of the lifter, grasp a bar (or other similar object) with your hands slightly wider than shoulder-width apart and place one foot in front of the other.

**Lifter:** Stand in front of the spotter, grasp the bar with your hands approximately shoulder-width apart (inside the spotter's grip), position your elbows close to the sides of your torso, keep your wrists and back flat and spread your feet apart a comfortable distance. To do the exercise, keep your elbows against your sides and pull the bar underneath your chin.

**Training Guideline (lifter):** Keep your torso in an upright position without bending backward at the waist as you perform this exercise.

## INCLINE BICEP

Start/Finish

Mid-point

**Muscle Worked:** biceps

**Suggested Repetitions:** 6 - 12 (or 40 - 70 seconds)

**Spotter:** Stand near the lifter's right side and place your right hand flat near her right wrist.

**Lifter:** Straighten your right arm, place it on the back pad of an incline bench and open your right hand. To do the exercise, pull your right hand toward your chin while keeping your right wrist flat. Repeat the exercise for the other side of your body.

**Training Guideline (lifter):** Relax your shoulders as you perform this exercise.

## BACK EXTENSION

**Start/Finish**

**Mid-point**

**Muscle Worked:** erector spinae, gluteus maximus and hamstrings

**Suggested Repetitions:** 10 - 15 (or 60 - 90 seconds)

**Spotter:** Stand in front of the lifter and place your hands flat on her upper back.

**Lifter:** Position your pelvis on the hip pad(s) of a back-extension bench, place your lower legs between the roller pads, let your torso hang straight down and fold your arms across your chest. To do the exercise, raise your torso until it's approximately parallel to the floor.

**Training Guideline (lifter):** Get a full stretch at the end of each repetition as you perform this exercise.

## HIP ABDUCTION

**Start/Finish**

**Mid-point**

**Muscles Worked:** gluteus medius and tensor fasciae latae

**Suggested Repetitions:** 10 - 15 (or 60 - 90 seconds)

**Spotter:** Kneel behind the lifter near her hips and place your right hand on the left side of her abdomen and your left hand just above her left knee.

**Lifter:** Lie on the floor on your right side in front of the spotter, position your head on your right arm, look straight ahead, straighten your legs and point your toes forward. To do the exercise, raise your left leg as high as possible. Repeat the exercise for the other side of your body.

**Training Guideline (lifter):** Keep your hips stationary without rotating forward or backward as you perform this exercise.

## HIP ADDUCTION

**Start/Finish**

**Mid-point**

**Muscles Worked:** hip adductors (adductor magnus, adductor longus, adductor brevis, pectineus and gracilis)

**Suggested Repetitions:** 10 - 15 (or 60 - 90 seconds)

**Spotter:** Kneel in front of the lifter and place your lower arms on the insides of her thighs just above her knees.

**Lifter:** Sit on the floor in front of the lifter, lean back, position your hands on the floor slightly behind your hips, place the soles of your feet together, bring your feet toward your hips and spread your knees apart. To do the exercise, bring your knees together.

**Training Guideline (lifter):** Keep your back straight as you perform this exercise.

## HIP FLEXION

Start/Finish

Mid-point

**Muscles Worked:** iliopsoas and transversus abdominis

**Suggested Repetitions:** 10 - 15 (or 60 - 90 seconds)

**Spotter:** Position your feet alongside the lifter's chest (while facing her legs) and place your hands near (or on) her knees.

**Lifter:** Lie supine on the floor between the spotter's feet, raise your head, wrap your arms around her lower legs, keep your back flat, straighten your legs, put your feet together and point your toes. To do the exercise, bring your knees toward your chest until your upper legs are approximately perpendicular to the floor.

**Training Guideline (lifter):** Keep your abdominals tight, focus on driving your knees and keep your feet off the floor as you perform this exercise.

## LEG CURL

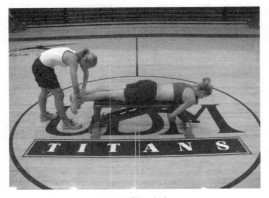

**Start/Finish**

**Mid-point**

**Muscle Worked:** hamstrings

**Suggested Repetitions:** 10 - 15 (or 60 - 90 seconds)

**Spotter:** Stand near the lifter's feet and place your hands against her heels.

**Lifter:** Lie prone on a bench and straighten your legs. To do the exercise, bring your heels toward your hips until the angle between your upper and lower legs is about 90 degrees or less.

**Training Guideline (lifter):** Keep your hips down as you perform this exercise.

## LEG EXTENSION

**Start/Finish**

**Mid-point**

**Muscle Worked:** quadriceps

**Suggested Repetitions:** 10 - 15 (or 60 - 90 seconds)

**Spotter:** Kneel in front of the lifter and place your right hand on her right upper leg just above her knee and your left hand on her right lower leg just above her ankle.

**Lifter:** Sit down on a bench, lean against the back pad (if one is available), position your right upper leg on the seat pad and let your right lower leg hang straight down. To do the exercise, straighten your right leg. Repeat the exercise for the other side of your body.

**Training Guideline (lifter):** Sit tall and keep your torso against the back pad (if one is available) as you perform this exercise.

## DORSI FLEXION

**Start/Finish**

**Mid-point**

**Muscle Worked:** anterior tibialis

**Suggested Repetitions:** 10 - 15 (or 60 - 90 seconds)

**Spotter:** Stand in front of the lifter and place your hands flat against the tops of her feet.

**Lifter:** Sit on a bench, lean back, position your hands on the back pad slightly behind your hips, straighten your legs and place them on the pad and position your heels so that they hang just over the edge of the pad. To do the exercise, pull your toes toward your torso.

**Training Guideline (lifter):** Sit tall, keep your leg straight and rotate at the ankle joint as you perform this exercise.

## FINAL THOUGHTS

In summary, MR can be very efficient and effective in any situation that might be encountered. Remember, an athlete can attain great results by using machines, free weights or MR. Although some teaching and instruction is required for MR, the time spent is well worth the results that can be achieved.

## REFERENCES

D'Amato, T. 2001. *Manual resistance - a productive alternative.* Available at http://www.naturalstrength.com.

Haney, M. 1997. *Manual resistance training can be creative, time efficient and productive alternative to conventional training.* Available at http://www.fitnessworld.com.

# 6

# A Sensible Look at Core Training

*Scott Savor, B.S.*

The core region consists of the trunk and pelvis which are used for maintaining the stability of the spine and pelvis (Allen et al. 2002). The anterior (front) mid-section is comprised of the abdominal muscles (the rectus abdominis, transversus abdominis, internal obliques and external obliques). These muscles produce torso flexion, lateral flexion and torso rotation. The posterior (back) mid-section is comprised of the transversocostal muscles (including the erector spinae), the transversospinalis muscles (the multifidus, rotares, semispinalis, interspinales and intertransversarii) and the quadratus lumborum. These muscles produce torso extension, lateral flexion and torso rotation (Mannie 2001).

Many individuals think that the most important region of the body is the core, especially in athletics. The theory behind this is that all athletic movements occur with the assistance of the abdominals and lower back. With respect to this, many authorities believe that an athlete is only as strong as her weakest muscular link (Pyle 2003). But with all that being said, does this mean that an athlete should emphasize her core region over other areas of her body?

Throughout the years, many variations have emerged on how to strengthen the core muscles. Examining the workouts of professional organizations, universities, high schools, personal-training centers, sportsmedical facilities and physical-therapy settings would reveal that core training can vary substantially. That's why it's important to investigate the practicality and sensibility behind what type of protocol is being done and why.

## A CLOSER LOOK

Generally speaking, there are many misconceptions within the field of strength training. Therefore, it's crucial to have a rhyme and a reason for implementing a certain approach.

Figure 6.1 shows an example of an anonymous – albeit an actual – core-training workout. Looking at this workout from several different perspectives will show whether or not the workout is sensible. Specifically, does the workout contain balance and symmetry throughout?

First, note that there's an overabundance of exercises for anterior mid-section (the abdominals) and only a handful for the posterior mid-section (the lower back). So, the approach being implemented implies that the abdominals are more important than the lower back. Also, why are two sets performed on some exercises and others only one? Let it be known that once emphasis is placed upon training a certain region of the body, another region is being neglected – possibly creating a muscular imbalance.

Second, how much volume is enough? Are the 24 - 29 sets that are prescribed for a "beginning" athlete a reasonable number of exercises for her core region? And what about the 27 - 39 exercises for an "advanced" athlete? On another note, does this leave an athlete with enough time to strengthen the other regions of her body? How much time is being wasted on unnecessary sets and repetitions? Mannie (2001) suggests that intensity is a major component in the human-performance equation. Keep in mind that the more exercises an athlete performs, the less intense she is. Couldn't the time that's devoted to all that core training be used more effectively to work on skill development, proper nutrition or recovery? Remember, balance is very important regardless of the sport or objective.

| EXERCISE | BEGINNING (Sets x Reps) | INTERMEDIATE (Sets x Reps) | ADVANCED (Sets x Reps) |
|---|---|---|---|
| Abdominal Twist | 2 x 10-15 | 2 x 15-20 | 2-3 x 20-25 |
| Oblique Lift | 2 x 10-15 | 2 x 15-20 | 2-4 x 20-25 |
| Bicycle | 2 x 10-15 (each side) | 2 x 15-20 (each side) | 1 x 40-50 |
| Flutter Kick | 2 x 10 | 2 x 15-20 | 2 x 20-25 |
| V-Sit | 1-2 x 5-10 | 2 x 10-15 | 2 x 15-30 |
| Abdominal Curl | 2 x 10-15 | 2 x 15-20 | 2-4 x 20-25 |
| Back Extension | 1-2 x 5-8 | 2 x 8-15 | 2-3 x 15-20 |
| Superman | 1 x 10-12 | 2 x 12-15 | 2-3 x 15-20 |
| Push-Up | 2 x 5-10 | 2 x 10-20 | 2-3 x 20-30 |
| Dip | 1-2 x 5-10 | 2 x 10-20 | 2-3 x 20-25 |
| Dead Bug | 2 x 10-12 | 2 x 12-20 | 2-4 x 20+ |
| Side Plank | 2 x 5 | 2 x 10-12 | 2 x 15+ |
| Quadruped Plank | 2 x 5 | 2 x 10-12 | 2 x 15+ |
| Body Bridge | 2-3 x 15 sec | 2-3 x 15-30 sec | 2-3 x 30+ sec |

**FIGURE 6.1: EXAMPLE OF A TRADITIONAL CORE-TRAINING WORKOUT**

## GENERAL GUIDELINES

An athlete should do all of her repetitions using this cadence: at least a two-second concentric (raising) phase, a brief pause in the contracted (or midpoint) position and at least a four-second eccentric (lowering) phase. Utilizing this speed of movement will minimize the involvement of momentum. In order to obtain the maximum possible results, the muscle(s) should be trained to the point of muscular fatigue or "failure" (when no further repetitions can be done with good form) within a repetition range of about 6 - 12 or a time frame of about 40 - 70 seconds.

It's also important to note that, ideally, core training should be done at or near the end of a workout. The reasoning behind this is that the core muscles act as stabilizers during other exercises. Thus, it's essential that the core muscles aren't pre-fatigued so that all exercises are *maximized* and the risk of injury is *minimized*.

In terms of volume, an athlete need only include 3 - 4 core exercises in her regular workout. The exercises can be varied as needed to prevent boredom and allow for personal preferences.

## THE EXERCISES

This chapter will describe the safest and most productive exercises that can be performed for the core region. Included in the discussions of each exercise are the muscle(s) worked (if more than one muscle is involved, the first muscle listed is the prime mover); suggested repetitions (the time that the targeted muscles should be loaded is shown in parentheses); brief but specific instructions as to how the spotter and lifter should perform the exercise; and training guidelines for the lifter to make the exercise safer and more productive. (Note: It's always advantageous to train with a partner or spotter. An effective partner can provide external motivation and aid in improving the intensity and quality of an exercise. This can result in better gains and faster results. But the reality is that an athlete might not always have someone with whom she can train. As a result, some of the following exercises don't require a spotter. In photographs that show two athletes, the lifter is wearing a dark top and the spotter is wearing a white top.)

The 15 exercises described in this chapter are 90 degree, wheel barrel, crunch, crunch (with ball), knee tuck, pendulum, oblique twist (bench), oblique twist (bar), bicycle, partner abs, body bridge, clock walk, lateral crawl, superman and kneeling alternate.

## 90 DEGREE

**Start/Finish**

**Mid-point**

**Muscle Worked:** rectus abdominis

**Suggested Repetitions:** 6 - 12 (or 40 - 70 seconds)

**Spotter:** Sit gently on the lifter's lower legs and place your feet alongside her hips.

**Lifter:** Lie supine on the floor, place the backs of your lower legs on a bench, position your body so that the angle between your upper and lower legs is approximately 90 degrees, fold your arms across your chest and raise your head. To do the exercise, bring your torso toward your legs.

**Training Guideline (lifter):** Lower your torso to the point where you touch the floor with the bottom part of your shoulder blades as you perform this exercise.

## WHEEL BARREL

Start/Finish

Mid-point

**Muscle Worked:** rectus abdominis

**Suggested Repetitions:** 6 - 12 (or 40 - 70 seconds)

**Spotter:** Stand near the lifter's feet and grasp her heels such that they're approximately 12 inches off the floor.

**Lifter:** Lie supine on the floor, straighten your legs, place your heels on the spotter's hands, fold your arms across your chest and raise your head. To do the exercise, bring your torso toward your legs but stop short of the point where it's perpendicular to the floor.

**Training Guideline (lifter):** Lower your torso to the point where you touch the floor with the bottom part of your shoulder blades as you perform this exercise.

## CRUNCH

**Start/Finish**

**Mid-point**

**Muscle Worked:** rectus abdominis

**Suggested Repetitions:** 6 - 12 (or 40 - 70 seconds)

**Spotter:** not required for this exercise

**Lifter:** Lie supine on the floor, bend your knees, place your feet flat on the floor, bring your legs together, fold your arms across your chest and raise your head. To do the exercise, bring your torso toward your legs but stop short of the point where it's perpendicular to the floor.

**Training Guideline (lifter):** Lower your torso to the point where you touch the floor with the bottom part of your shoulder blades as you perform this exercise.

## CRUNCH (with ball)

Start/Finish

Mid-point

**Muscle Worked:** rectus abdominis

**Suggested Repetitions:** 6 - 12 (or 40 - 70 seconds)

**Spotter:** not required for this exercise

**Lifter:** Lie supine on a stability ball so that it's under your lower back, bend your knees so that the angle between your upper and lower legs is about 90 degrees, place your feet flat on the floor and spread them apart a comfortable distance, fold your arms across your chest and raise your head. To do the exercise, bring your torso toward your legs.

**Training Guideline (lifter):** Keep your arms folded across your chest and bring your torso forward as much as possible as you perform this exercise.

## KNEE TUCK

**Start/Finish**

**Mid-point**

**Muscle Worked:** rectus abdominis and iliopsoas

**Suggested Repetitions:** 6 - 12 (or 40 - 70 seconds)

**Spotter:** not required for this exercise

**Lifter:** Assume a push-up position with your arms straight and your hands on the floor just below your shoulders, straighten your body and place your lower legs on a stability ball. To do the exercise, bring your knees toward your torso until the angle between your upper and lower legs is about 90 degrees or less.

**Training Guideline (lifter):** Maintain a stable base of support as you perform this exercise.

## PENDULUM

Start/Finish

Mid-point

**Muscle Worked:** internal obliques, external obliques, transversus abdominis and hip adductors

**Suggested Repetitions:** 6 - 12 (or 40 - 70 seconds)

**Spotter:** Stand behind the lifter's hips and spread your feet apart a comfortable distance.

**Lifter:** Lie supine on the floor, straighten your legs and raise them so that they're perpendicular to your torso, place a stability ball between your lower legs and position your hands flat on the floor away from your sides. To do the exercise, rotate your legs from side to side while keeping your shoulders flat on the floor.

**Training Guideline (lifter):** Use your arms to stabilize your body and lower the ball to the side without touching the floor or the spotter as you perform this exercise.

## OBLIQUE TWIST (bench)

**Start/Finish**

**Mid-point**

**Muscles Worked:** internal obliques, external obliques and transversus abdominis

**Suggested Repetitions:** 6 - 12 (or 40 - 70 seconds)

**Spotter:** not required for this exercise

**Lifter:** Lie on your right side on a bench, wrap your legs tightly underneath it, position your body so that your torso extends over its edge and fold your arms across your chest. To do the exercise, raise and rotate your torso from side to side but stop short of the point where it's perpendicular to the floor.

**Training Guideline (lifter):** Raise and rotate your torso as high as possible as you perform this exercise.

## OBLIQUE TWIST (bar)

**Start/Finish**

**Mid-point**

**Muscles Worked:** internal obliques, external obliques and transversus abdominis

**Suggested Repetitions:** 6 - 12 (or 40 - 70 seconds)

**Spotter:** Stand in front of the lifter, grasp a bar with your hands spaced slightly wider than shoulder-width apart, straighten your arms and spread your feet apart a comfortable distance.

**Lifter:** Stand in front of the spotter, grasp the bar with your hands spaced about shoulder-width apart (inside the spotter's grip), straighten your arms and spread your feet apart a comfortable distance. To do the exercise, rotate your torso from side to side while keeping your feet and hips as stationary as possible.

**Training Guideline (lifter):** Attempt to rotate your torso approximately 90 degrees (in each direction) as you perform this exercise.

## BICYCLE

**Start/Finish**

**Mid-point**

**Muscles Worked:** internal obliques, external obliques and transversus abdominis

**Suggested Repetitions:** 6 - 12 (or 40 - 70 seconds)

**Spotter:** not required for this exercise

**Lifter:** Lie supine on the floor, raise your shoulders, place your hands behind your head, straighten one leg and bend the other. To do the exercise, rotate your torso from side to side by bringing an elbow to the opposite knee.

**Training Guideline (lifter):** Avoid pulling on your head as you perform this exercise.

## PARTNER ABS

Start/Finish

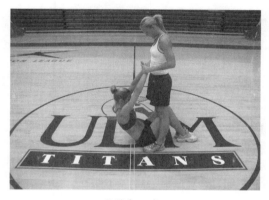

Mid-point

**Muscle Worked:** transversus abdominis

**Suggested Repetitions:** 6 - 12 (or 40 - 70 seconds)

**Spotter:** Stand with your feet alongside the lifter's hips (while facing her head), squeeze her knees together and place your hands on her wrists.

**Lifter:** Lie supine on the floor, straighten your arms, put your hands together, bend your knees, place your feet flat on the floor and raise your head. To do the exercise, allow the spotter to raise your torso toward your legs and then resist as she pushes you back to the floor.

**Training Guideline (lifter):** Let the spotter do the positive (raising) phase and then resist her in the negative (lowering) phase as you perform this exercise.

## BODY BRIDGE

**Start/Finish**

**Mid-point**

**Muscle Worked:** transversus abdominis and erector spinae

**Suggested Repetitions:** 6 - 12 (or 40 - 70 seconds)

**Spotter:** not required for this exercise

**Lifter:** Lie prone on the floor, place your forearms flat, bend your arms so that the angle between your upper and lower arms is approximately 90 degrees, straighten your legs and bring them together. To do the exercise, elevate your hips until your torso is approximately parallel to the floor and maintain that position.

**Training Guideline (lifter):** Avoid raising or lowering your hips so that your torso remains approximately parallel to the floor as you perform this exercise.

## CLOCK WALK

Start/Finish

Mid-point

**Muscles Worked:** transversus abdominis, erector spinae, anterior deltoid, posterior deltoid, latissimus dorsi ("lats") and triceps

**Suggested Repetitions:** 10 - 15 (or 60 - 90 seconds)

**Spotter:** not required for this exercise

**Lifter:** Assume a push-up position with your arms straight and your hands on the floor just below your shoulders, straighten your body and place your toes on a bench. To do the exercise, "walk" your hands slowly to your right until your body is at a 9-o'clock position, then "walk" your hands quickly to your left until your body is at a 3-o'clock position.

**Training Guideline (lifter):** Keep your body straight as you perform this exercise.

## LATERAL CRAWL

**Start/Finish**

**Mid-point**

**Muscles Worked:** transversus abdominis, erector spinae, posterior deltoid, latissimus dorsi ("lats"), gluteus medius, tensor fasciae latae and triceps

**Suggested Time:** approximately 3 - 5 minutes

**Spotter:** not required for this exercise

Lifter: Assume a push-up position with your arms straight, your hands on the floor spaced approximately shoulder-width apart, your feet spread slightly and your heels and hips raised. To do the exercise, reach up, out and over with your left arm and left leg simultaneously and then alternate.

**Training Guideline (lifter):** Keep your body in a stable position as you perform this exercise.

## SUPERMAN

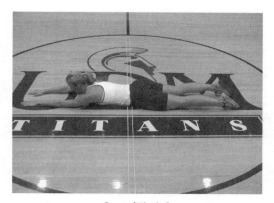

**Start/Finish**

**Mid-point**

**Muscles Worked:** erector spinae, anterior deltoid, posterior deltoid and gluteus maximus

**Suggested Repetitions:** 6 - 12 (or 40 - 70 seconds)

**Spotter:** not required for this exercise

**Lifter:** Lie prone on the floor with your arms extended past your head and your legs straight. To do the exercise, raise your arms and legs as high as possible.

**Training Guideline (lifter):** Keep your arms extended and your legs straight with your toes pointed as you perform this exercise.

## KNEELING ALTERNATE

**Start/Finish**

**Mid-point**

**Muscles Worked:** erector spinae, anterior deltoid, posterior deltoid and gluteus maximus

**Suggested Repetitions:** 6 - 12 (or 40 - 70 seconds)

**Spotter:** not required for this exercise

**Lifter:** Position yourself on the floor on your hands and knees with your hands spaced approximately shoulder-width apart and your arms and upper legs perpendicular to the floor. To do the exercise, simultaneously raise your right arm and left leg as high as possible and then alternate.

**Training Guideline (lifter):** Keep your arms and legs straight with your toes pulled forward as you perform this exercise.

With the exception of bodybuilding, no athletic competition in the world has been won by a pose-down contest. (Photo by Scott Savor)

## FINAL THOUGHTS

With the exception of bodybuilding, no athletic competition in the world has been won by a pose-down contest. It's very important that an athlete's objective should be to train her core region very intensely with balance and symmetry. An athlete should approach her low-back training in the same way as her abdominal-training.

Core training has become very popular in the realm of strength training and athletics. Certainly, training the core is essential in maximizing athletic performance. However, it's critical that no musculature is emphasized over another unless it's to minimize the risk of injury during athletic participation. Quite often, athletes perform numerous extra sets/reps for the abdominal region in an effort to achieve "six-pack abs" or have some other type of unrealistic agenda that's totally unrelated to increasing her performance potential or decreasing her injury potential. When this occurs, an imbalance is being developed thus possibly increasing her risk of injury within that specific region of her body.

Keep in mind that an athlete needs to train the muscles of her core just as intensely as she trains her pectorals, latissimus dorsi, quadriceps and every other muscle. There's no scientific research that states the abdominals – or any other muscle group – are more important than the hamstrings, dorsi flexors, quadriceps, deltoids or any other muscle. Similar to any other type of training, core training should be reasonable and sensible: The objective should be – and always be – balance and symmetry throughout the body which is vital in the prevention of injuries and maximization of athletic potential.

## REFERENCES

Allen, S., G. A. Dudley, M. Iosia, B. Steuerwald and D. Stanforth. 2002. Core strength training. *Sports Science Exchange Roundtable* 47 (13): n1.

Mannie, K. 2001. Core training. *Coach and Athletic Director* 71 (i2): 6.

Pyle, S. 2003. *Core strength training. Multi-sport coaching.* Available at http://www.tri-coach.com/art5.htm.

# 7

# Reducing the Risk of Injury in Women's Sports

*Matt Brzycki, B.S.*

Rebecca Lobo was one of the most dominant female basketball players of her era. In four years at the University of Connecticut (1991-95), she scored 2,133 points and grabbed 1,268 rebounds. During those four years, Lobo led her team to a record of 106-25 which included a 35-0 record and a National Collegiate Athletic Association (NCAA) Championship in 1995. She was the youngest member of the United States Olympic Team that won a gold medal in the 1996 Olympics in Atlanta.

As further testament to her athletic ability, Lobo was the second player ever signed by the Women's Basketball Association (WNBA). In her first two seasons with the New York Liberty (1997-98), she played in a total of 58 regular-season games, averaging almost 31.3 minutes per game. With an average of about 12.03 points and 7.07 rebounds per game during those two seasons, Lobo had a bright future. Only 42 seconds into the 1999 season opener against the Cleveland Rockers in Madison Square Garden, she tore her anterior cruciate ligament (ACL). After two surgeries and two years of rehabilitation, Lobo returned to the WNBA but was never the same player. In her next three seasons (2001-03), she played in a total of 62 regular-season games, averaging about 8.3 minutes per game. During those three seasons, her scoring and rebounding averages plummeted to about 1.75 points and 1.43 rebounds per game. In 2003, Rebecca Lobo retired from the WNBA after an injury-plagued professional career in which she played in only 55% of her team's regular-season games (121 of 220). Who knows what she might've accomplished if she hadn't been plagued by knee injuries?

Of course, this story of unfulfilled potential because of injuries isn't the only one. The fact of the matter is that for any athlete – male or female – injuries are an unforeseen, inevitable and unfortunate fact of life. Generally speaking, an injury occurs when an outside force momentarily exceeds the integrity of a structural element – such as a muscle, bone and/or connective tissues – so that it's aggressively stretched or moved beyond its existing range of motion.

The upcoming information will discuss ways to reduce the risk of injury. But first, it's necessary to understand the extent of injuries in women's sports.

## INJURIES IN SELECTED SPORTS

In 1982, the NCAA developed its Injury Surveillance System (ISS) to provide data on injury trends in intercollegiate athletics. Each year, injury data are collected from a representative sample of NCAA member institutions. Although the data on injuries were gathered from collegiate athletes, the information is also quite applicable and useful to high-school coaches and athletes.

Currently, data are accumulated on eight women's sports: basketball, field hockey, gymnastics, ice hockey, lacrosse, soccer, softball and volleyball. The data are published annually in reports that contain an enormous amount of material – far too much to be discussed within the confines of this chapter. As such, a small sampling of data for the eight women's sports is presented here.

Before introducing the data, it's important to define a few terms. The first one is "injury." In order to be counted as an "injury" in the ISS, three criteria must be met:

1. It occurs as a result of participation in an organized intercollegiate practice or contest.

2. It requires medical attention by a team athletic trainer or physician.

3. It results in restriction of the student-athlete's participation for one or more days beyond the day of injury.

It's also important to become familiar with a unique term that's mentioned repeatedly in the reports: athlete exposure (or A-E). In the ISS, an athlete exposure is defined as "one athlete participating in one practice or game where he or she is exposed to the possibility of athletic injury." Example: 10 basketball games that involved 20 athletes per game would result in 200 athlete exposures [10 games x 20 A-Es/game = 200 A-Es].

The final term that must be understood is "injury rate." In the ISS, the injury rate is defined as "a ratio of the number of injuries in a particular category to the number of athlete exposures in that category." Also of importance is the fact that in the ISS, the injury rates are expressed per 1,000 athlete exposures. So a game injury rate of 10.0 would mean that there were 10.0 injuries per 1,000 athlete exposures. Example: In 50 basketball games that involved 20 athletes per game (1,000 athlete exposures), it would be expected that 10.0 injuries would occur – or one injury every five games.

What follows is bulleted information that was gleaned from the ISS data for the eight women's sports that were mentioned earlier. (Unless otherwise noted, the data are for the 2002-03 season.)

## Basketball

The ISS has tracked women's basketball since the 1988-89 season. The injury data include the following:

- 65.7% of all injuries occurred in practices; 34.3% of all injuries occurred in games.

- The top three body parts injured during practices were the ankle, knee and foot. They accounted for about 50% of all reported injuries.

- The top three body parts injured during games were the knee, ankle and head. They accounted for about 62% of all reported injuries.
- The top three types of injuries during practices were sprains, strains and contusions.
- The top three types of injuries during games were sprains, contusions and concussions.
- From 1988-2003 (15 seasons), the practice injury rate was 4.6. (From 1988-2003, the practice injury rate was 4.3 in men's basketball.)
- From 1988-2003, the game injury rate was 9.0. (From 1988-2003, the game injury rate was 10.0 in men's basketball.)
- From 1988-2003, the game injury rate on a wooden surface was 9.0; the game injury rate on a composite surface was 8.6.

## Field Hockey

The ISS has tracked field hockey since the 1986-87 season. The injury data include the following:

- 64.9% of all injuries occurred in practices; 35.1% of all injuries occurred in games.
- The top three body parts injured during practices were the upper leg, ankle and pelvis/hips. They accounted for about 38% of all reported injuries.
- The top three body parts injured during games were the head, ankle and knee. They accounted for about 35% of all reported injuries.
- The top three types of injuries during practices were strains, sprains and tendinitis.
- The top three types of injuries during games were strains, sprains and contusions.
- From 1986-2003 (17 seasons), the practice injury rate was 4.0.
- From 1986-2003, the game injury rate was 8.4.
- From 1988-2003 (15 seasons), the game injury rate on a natural surface was 8.6; the game injury rate on an artificial surface was 8.5.

## Gymnastics

The ISS has tracked women's gymnastics since the 1985-86 season. The injury data include the following:

- 86.4% of all injuries occurred in practices; 13.6% of all injuries occurred in meets.
- The top three body parts injured during practices were the ankle, knee and foot. They accounted for about 44% of all reported injuries.
- The top three body parts injured during meets were the knee, ankle and elbow. They accounted for about 67% of all reported injuries.

- The top three types of injuries during practices were sprains, strains and fractures.
- The top three types of injuries during meets were sprains, hyperextensions and contusions.
- During practices, 38% of the injuries occurred on the floor exercise, 17% on the balance beam, 14% on the uneven bars and 14% on the vault. (17% of the injuries occurred during "other" activities and the warm-up.)
- During meets, 46% of the injuries occurred on the vault, 27% on the uneven bars, 7% on the floor exercise and 7% on the balance beam. (13% of the injuries occurred during the warm-up.)
- From 1985-2003 (18 seasons), the practice injury rate was 7.3.
- From 1985-2003, the meet injury rate was 17.8.

## Ice Hockey

The ISS has tracked women's ice hockey since the 2000-01 season. The injury data include the following:

- 41.8% of all injuries occurred in practices; 58.2% of all injuries occurred in games.
- The top three body parts injured during practices were the head, shoulder and knee. They accounted for about 42% of all reported injuries.
- The top three body parts injured during games were the head, knee and shoulder. They accounted for about 55% of all reported injuries.
- The top three types of injuries during practices were strains, contusions and concussions.
- The top three types of injuries during games were concussions, sprains and contusions.
- From 2000-03 (3 seasons), the practice injury rate was 2.7. (From 1986-2003, the practice injury rate was 2.2 in men's ice hockey.)
- From 2000-03, the game injury rate was 13.0. (From 1986-2003, the game injury rate was 17.4 in men's ice hockey.)

## Lacrosse

The ISS has tracked women's lacrosse since the 1986-87 season. The injury data include the following:

- 67.5% of all injuries occurred in practices; 32.5% of all injuries occurred in games.
- The top three body parts injured during practices were the ankle, lower leg and upper leg. They accounted for about 46% of all reported injuries.
- The top three body parts injured during games were the ankle, knee and head. They accounted for about 58% of all reported injuries.

- The top three types of injuries during practices were sprains, strains and stress fractures.
- The top three types of injuries during games were sprains, contusions and strains.
- From 1986-2003 (17 seasons), the practice injury rate was 3.6. (From 1987-2003, the practice injury rate was 3.6 in men's lacrosse.)
- From 1986-2003, the game injury rate was 7.6. (From 1987-2003, the game injury rate was 14.5 in men's lacrosse.)
- From 1986-2003, the game injury rate on a natural surface was 7.0; the game injury rate on an artificial surface was 8.0.

## Soccer

The ISS has tracked women's soccer since the 1986-87 season. The injury data include the following:
- 51.5% of all injuries occurred in practices; 48.5% of all injuries occurred in games.
- The top three body parts injured during practices were the upper leg, ankle and knee. They accounted for about 62% of all reported injuries.
- The top three body parts injured during games were the ankle, knee and head. They accounted for about 63% of all reported injuries.
- The top three types of injuries during practices were strains, sprains and tendinitis.
- The top three types of injuries during games were sprains, contusions and strains.
- From 1986-2003 (17 seasons), the practice injury rate was 5.6. (From 1986-2003, the practice injury rate was 4.6 in men's soccer.)
- From 1986-2003, the game injury rate was 17.4. (From 1986-2003, the game injury rate was 20.0 in men's soccer.)
- From 1988-2003 (15 seasons), the game injury rate on a natural surface was 17.8; the game injury rate on an artificial surface was 18.0.

## Softball

The ISS has tracked softball since the 1986-87 season. The injury data include the following:
- 47.3% of all injuries occurred in practices; 52.7% of all injuries occurred in games.
- The top three body parts injured during practices were the shoulder, knee and ankle. They accounted for about 45% of all reported injuries.
- The top three body parts injured during games were the ankle, knee and head. They accounted for about 36% of all reported injuries.

- The top three types of injuries during practices were strains, sprains and contusions.
- The top three types of injuries during games were sprains, contusions and fractures.
- From 1986-2003 (17 seasons), the practice injury rate was 3.1. (From 1985-2003, the practice injury rate was 2.1 in baseball.)
- From 1986-2003, the game injury rate was 4.8. (From 1985-2003, the game injury rate was 6.1 in baseball.)
- From 1988-2003 (15 seasons), the game injury rate on a natural surface was 2.4; the game injury rate on an artificial surface was 3.6.

## Volleyball

The ISS has tracked volleyball since the 1984-85 season. The injury data include the following:

- 65.6% of all injuries occurred in practices; 34.4% of all injuries occurred in games.
- The top three body parts injured during practices were the ankle, shoulder and knee. They accounted for about 43% of all reported injuries.
- The top three body parts injured during games were the ankle, knee and shoulder. They accounted for about 59% of all reported injuries.
- The top three types of injuries during practices were strains, sprains and "other."
- The top three types of injuries during games were sprains, strains and contusions.
- From 1985-2003 (18 seasons), the practice injury rate was 4.4.
- From 1985-2003, the game injury rate was 4.8.
- From 1988-2003 (15 seasons), the game injury rate on a wooden surface was 4.8; the game injury rate on a composite surface was 4.5.

## IMPLICATIONS

Tables 7.1 and 7.2 summarize the data concerning the top three body parts injured and the top three types of injuries for all eight sports during the 2002-03 season, respectively. From this summary, it's clear that the types of injuries that occur the most in the eight sports are sprains and strains and, to a lesser degree, contusions (or, simply, bruises).

In order to reduce the potential for injury, an athlete must prepare her body for the rigors of competition by engaging in a comprehensive and progressive training program. In a nutshell, she must improve her body's capacity to tolerate stress from an outside force. If her muscles, bones and connective tissues can tolerate more stress, she'll be less susceptible to injury. This doesn't mean that an athlete who prepares herself for competition will never get hurt.

| Sport | TOP THREE BODY PARTS INJURED | |
| --- | --- | --- |
| | In Practice | In Competition |
| Basketball | ankle - 25% | knee- 28% |
| | knee - 17% | ankle - 22% |
| | foot - 8% | head - 12% |
| Field Hockey | upper leg - 16% | head - 12% |
| | ankle - 11% | ankle - 12% |
| | pelvis, hips - 11% | knee - 11% |
| Gymnastics | ankle - 18% | knee - 47% |
| | knee - 18% | ankle - 13% |
| | foot - 8% | elbow - 7% |
| Ice Hockey | head - 18% | head - 28% |
| | shoulder - 12% | knee - 14% |
| | knee - 12% | shoulder - 13% |
| Lacrosse | ankle - 19% | ankle - 23% |
| | lower leg - 15% | knee - 23% |
| | upper leg - 12% | head - 12% |
| Soccer | upper leg - 25% | ankle - 31% |
| | ankle  - 21% | knee - 20% |
| | knee - 16% | head - 12% |
| Softball | shoulder - 20% | ankle - 15% |
| | knee - 14% | knee - 12% |
| | ankle - 11% | head - 9% |
| Volleyball | ankle - 18% | ankle - 31% |
| | shoulder - 14% | knee - 14% |
| | knee - 11% | shoulder - 14% |

**TABLE 7.1: THE TOP THREE BODY PARTS INJURED DURING PRACTICE AND COMPETITION IN EIGHT WOMEN'S SPORTS**

Many injuries are the result of being in the wrong place at the wrong time. However, a training program will certainly reduce the risk. In addition, having structural elements that are more resilient to outside forces will reduce the severity of any injury that an athlete may sustain and allow her to return from an injury more quickly.

Training should focus on the larger muscles of the body with special attention given to those that affect body parts that are most likely to get injured. For instance, preparation for every sport should emphasize the muscles that influence the ankle and knee joints since those body parts are frequently injured; preparation for sports such as ice hockey, softball and volleyball should also emphasize the muscles that influence the shoulder joint. Though not mentioned in the data as body parts that are most often injured, attention should also be directed to the muscles that affect the lower back and elbow regardless of the sport.

| Sport | TOP THREE TYPES OF INJURIES | |
|---|---|---|
| | In Practice | In Competition |
| Basketball | sprain - 33% | sprain - 40% |
| | strain - 15% | contusion - 13% |
| | contusion - 7% | concussion - 11% |
| Field Hockey | strain - 37% | strain - 20% |
| | sprain - 15% | sprain - 19% |
| | tendinitis - 9% | contusion - 15% |
| Gymnastics | sprain - 37% | sprain - 60% |
| | strain - 17% | hyperextension - 20% |
| | fracture - 6% | contusion - 7% |
| Ice Hockey | strain - 24% | concussion - 28% |
| | contusion - 22% | sprain - 20% |
| | concussion - 18% | contusion - 14% |
| Lacrosse | sprain - 25% | sprain - 39% |
| | strain - 20% | contusion - 13% |
| | stress fracture - 9% | strain - 11% |
| Soccer | strain - 37% | sprain - 35% |
| | sprain - 25% | contusion - 19% |
| | tendinitis - 7% | strain - 14% |
| Softball | strain - 26% | sprain - 24% |
| | sprain - 17% | contusion - 21% |
| | contusion - 11% | fracture - 15% |
| Volleyball | strain - 30% | sprain - 46% |
| | sprain - 27% | strain - 14% |
| | other - 9% | contusion - 7% |

**TABLE 7.2: THE TOP THREE TYPES OF INJURIES DURING PRACTICE AND COMPETITION IN EIGHT WOMEN'S SPORTS**

## PREPARATION

An athlete can prepare herself for competition by aggressively and enthusiastically participating in four activities: strength training, conditioning, flexibility training and skill training. Here's a brief description of those activities:

### Strength Training

Increasing the strength of the muscles, bones and connective tissues will allow those structural elements to tolerate more stress. If the muscles, bones and connective tissues can tolerate more stress, the risk of injury will be reduced. While the importance of increasing muscular strength is widely accepted, there's no consensus as to the optimal way of doing so. Nor is there any shortage of opinions. The fact of the matter is that many programs can be effective despite being – in some cases – polar opposites. An athlete can increase her muscular strength by incorporating these basic guidelines:

- Exercise with an appropriate degree of intensity (or effort).
- Try to progress from one workout to the next by either increasing the amount of resistance that was used or improving upon the number of repetitions that was completed with the same resistance.
- Avoid doing the repetitions with an excessive amount of momentum.
- Perform each repetition throughout a full range of motion.
- Focus on the larger muscle groups in the body (the hips, legs and torso).
- Strengthen the muscles that surround the joints that are most likely to get injured in a particular sport.
- Exercise the muscles from largest to smallest (the hips, upper legs, lower legs, torso, upper arms, lower arms, abdominals and lower back).
- Take as little rest as possible between exercises/sets.
- Allow for adequate recovery between workouts.
- Keep track of performance in the weight room (resistance and repetitions).
- Train with a partner.

## Conditioning

Training for sports should involve aerobic and anaerobic conditioning. By increasing aerobic and anaerobic fitness, an athlete will surrender to fatigue less quickly. Being able to compete with less fatigue will reduce an athlete's risk of injury. An athlete can improve her level of conditioning by following these basic guidelines:

- Focus on aerobic conditioning – that is, continuous efforts of long duration such as long-distance running – to establish a solid foundation of aerobic support.
- Concentrate on anaerobic conditioning – that is, a series of all-out efforts of short duration such as sprints – as the competitive season nears (if it's applicable to the sport).
- Elevate the heart rate to levels that will stimulate a training response.
- Try to progress from one workout to the next by completing the same distance at a faster pace (in a shorter amount of time), covering a greater distance at the same pace or gradually increasing both the distance and the pace.
- Include some non-weightbearing activities in training – such as swimming and rowing – to reduce the risk of experiencing or complicating an orthopedic problem.

## Flexibility Training

By becoming more flexible, an athlete has increased the ranges of motion around her joints. Can this reduce her risk of injury? Perhaps. Consider an athlete who lacks flexibility in her hamstrings. If the hamstrings are forcefully stretched beyond their existing range of motion, she may strain the muscle – an injury that possibly could've been avoided if she had greater flexibility in her hamstrings. Flexibility is also an inherent aspect of several sports/activities such as gymnastics, diving, dance and figure skating. Moreover, greater flexibility gives an athlete the potential to produce and apply force over a greater distance. An athlete can increase her flexibility by following these basic guidelines:

- Precede flexibility training with a warm-up that results in a light sweat.
- Do the stretch under control without any bouncing, bobbing or jerking movements.
- Inhale and exhale normally during the stretch without holding the breath.
- Stretch comfortably in a pain-free manner.
- Relax during the stretch.
- Hold each stretch for about 30 - 60 seconds.

**Training should focus on the larger muscles of the body with special attention given to those that affect body parts that are most likely to get injured. (Photo by Pete Silletti)**

- Attempt to stretch a little bit farther than the last time.
- Stretch all of the major muscle groups in the body.
- Perform flexibility movements on a regular basis. (Note: For a detailed discussion of flexibility training, you're encouraged to read the chapter "Improving Flexibility" by Rachael Picone in *The Female Athlete: Train for Success*.)

## Skill Training

Learning and perfecting sport-specific skills and techniques allow an athlete to perform more efficiently. By being more efficient in the performance of her skills, an athlete will fatigue less quickly and be in greater control of her body. An athlete can develop her skills by following these basic guidelines:

- Learn how to do the skills correctly.
- Perform the skills over and over again until they can be executed without conscious effort.
- Practice the skills perfectly and exactly as they'd be used in the athletic arena.
- Avoid trying to simulate skills with barbells, dumbbells or other weighted equipment.

## BE PREPARED!

Preparation for competition should be a year-round endeavor – not just immediately prior to the season. During the season, it's especially critical that athletes engage in appropriate activities that improve their levels of strength, conditioning, flexibility and skill since this is the time when they need to maximize their performance.

What can female athletes do to reduce their risk of injury? The main thing is to be prepared!

*Note:* Conclusions drawn from or recommendations based on the data provided by the National Collegiate Athletic Association [NCAA] are those of the author based on analyses/evaluations of the author and do not represent the views of the officers, staff or membership of the NCAA.

## REFERENCES

National Collegiate Athletic Association [NCAA]. 2003. *Injury surveillance system women's basketball 2002-03.* Indianapolis, IN: NCAA.

_____. 2003. *Injury surveillance system field hockey 2002-03.* Indianapolis, IN: NCAA.

_____. 2003. *Injury surveillance system gymnastics 2002-03.* Indianapolis, IN: NCAA.

_____. 2003. *Injury surveillance system women's ice hockey 2002-03.* Indianapolis, IN: NCAA.

_____. 2003. *Injury surveillance system women's lacrosse 2002-03.* Indianapolis, IN: NCAA.

_____. 2003. *Injury surveillance system women's soccer 2002-03.* Indianapolis, IN: NCAA.

_____. 2003. *Injury surveillance system women's softball 2002-03.* Indianapolis, IN: NCAA.

_____. 2003. *Injury surveillance system women's volleyball 2002-03.* Indianapolis, IN: NCAA.

# 8

# Prescription for Rehabilitative Training

*Matt Brzycki, B.S.*

In general, injuries can be either traumatic or non-traumatic. Traumatic injuries are more serious and severe such as fractures of bone and tears of muscle or connective tissues. Quite often, these types of injuries require surgical intervention. On the other hand, non-traumatic injuries are less serious and severe such as tendinitis and bursitis. Sometimes, these kinds of injuries simply result from overuse. Regardless of the type of injury, it's important for an injured athlete to consult with a qualified sportsmedical specialist such as an orthopedic physician, physical therapist or athletic trainer.

## RATIONALE

In many instances, a female athlete who suffers an injury ends up eliminating all forms of conditioning – even those that involve uninjured body parts. Yet, it's extremely important to continue some type of conditioning whenever possible – even in the event of an injury. Many authorities have suggested that a muscle begins to lose size and strength if it doesn't receive an adequate amount of stimulation within 48 - 96 hours of a previous workout. There's some anecdotal evidence suggesting that it may be a bit longer than this time frame – at least for some individuals. But it's clear that a loss of muscular size and strength will occur after some period of extended inactivity. Moreover, the rate of strength loss is most rapid during the first few weeks. Because of this, rehabilitative training can prevent a significant loss of not only muscular size and strength but also aerobic and anaerobic fitness. This, of course, is provided that the training can be done in a pain-free – or nearly pain free – fashion.

Whether the injury is traumatic or non-traumatic, it will have some degree of impact upon an athlete's training. In fact, some injuries – especially those that are traumatic – might not permit any physical activity whatsoever. Nevertheless, an athlete can often train parts of her body that aren't related to the afflicted area. And in many cases, she may even be able to address the injured body part directly.

## PRUDENT METHODS

There are several different options and adjustments that an athlete can use to continue training an injured area or body part in a safe, sensible and pain-free manner. It should be noted that these methods aren't intended for injuries that are viewed as being very serious or extremely painful. As such, an athlete should receive approval from a certified sportsmedical authority before initiating any prescription for rehabilitative training. Ken Mannie, the Strength and Conditioning Coach at Michigan State University, suggests that the approval should also include a report of the specific nature and severity of the injury. This information should be relayed to the strength and fitness professional to determine an appropriate prescription.

Rehabilitative training can be performed by considering and then applying the following guidelines:

## 1. Lighten the weight.

If an athlete wants to continue training an injured body part in the weight room, her first step is to decrease the amount of resistance that she normally uses in exercises that involve the afflicted area. This is usually the easiest and most straightforward recommendation. Suppose that an athlete had a knee injury and, as a result, she experienced pain in her patellar tendon when doing the leg extension with her usual level of resistance. Decreasing the amount of weight will produce less stress on her tendon and perhaps allow the athlete to perform the exercise in a pain-free – or nearly pain-free – manner. The amount that the weight is reduced depends upon the extent and nature of her injury.

## 2. Slow the speed of movement.

Often done in conjunction with decreasing the amount of resistance for an exercise is using a slower speed of movement. Slowing the repetition speed will decrease the orthopedic stress placed upon a given joint. An athlete could, for example, do repetitions that are 20 seconds long when training an injured area by raising the weight in 10 seconds and lowering it in 10 seconds.

As the injury heals, the athlete can gradually return to her preferred speed of movement. Then again, she may find that the extra-slow speed of movement is more appealing and continue using it after she completes her rehabilitative training. Or perhaps she may even adopt the slower speed of movement to train other body parts that aren't injured. Incidentally, slowing down the speed of movement will also necessitate using a reduced amount of weight thereby lowering the orthopedic stress even further.

## 3. Change the exercise angle.

If pain persists during certain exercises that involve an injured body part, it may be possible for an athlete to change the angle of the exercise. Essentially, this alters – and restricts – the angle through which she moves her limbs.

This option can be used with many exercises for the torso – particularly those that involve the shoulder joint. This is especially important because the mobility and instability of the shoulder joint make it highly prone to injury. In fact, one of the most frequently injured body parts in many sports is the shoulder joint. A common problem in this joint is known as "shoulder-impingement syndrome" – a general term used to describe pain that's often characterized as "tightness" or "pinching" in the shoulder.

Slowing the repetition speed will decrease the orthopedic stress placed upon a given joint. (Photo by Pete Silletti)

Suppose that an athlete has slight shoulder impingement when doing a bench press. In some cases, if she changes the angle of the exercise from supine (flat) to decline – in other words, she changes from the bench press to the decline press – there's significantly less orthopedic stress on her shoulder joint.

Likewise, some athletes experience pain due to shoulder impingement when moving the bar behind their heads during the seated press and overhand lat pulldown. Generally speaking, the discomfort in both of these exercises can be lessened considerably by changing the angle of the push and pull. This can be done by performing the exercises with the bar traveling in front of the head rather than behind the neck.

This option has limited – but useful – applications for aerobic and anaerobic conditioning. If an athlete has low-back pain, for example, she can pedal a cycle in a recumbent position rather than an upright one. This angle offers greater support for her lower back thereby decreasing the amount of stress in her lumbar area.

## 4. Use a different grip or hand position.

Many times there's less orthopedic stress when a different grip or hand position is used. Once again, this is extremely relevant when addressing the oft-injured shoulder joint. If an athlete has a slight pain in her shoulder when doing an exercise such as the bench press, it's quite possible that she'll have a significant reduction in pain by simply changing the position of her hands from that used with a barbell to a "parallel grip" (that is, her palms facing each other) with dumbbells. In exercises for the torso, changing the position of the hand in this manner causes the head of the humerus (the upper-arm bone) to rotate laterally which may relieve the stress in the shoulder joint.

It should be noted that every exercise that can be performed with a barbell can also be performed with dumbbells. These exercises include the bench press, incline press, decline press, seated press, upright row, shoulder shrug, bicep curl, tricep extension and wrist flexion. As such, an athlete has an option for varying the position of her hands in exercises for just about every major muscle in her torso. Additionally, many machines allow an athlete to vary the position of her grip/hand at her convenience without any major loss of technique or function.

## 5. Perform different exercises.

Yet another option for rehabilitative training in the weight room is to perform different exercises that require the same muscle groups. For instance, if an athlete simply cannot perform any type of lat pulldown without experiencing shoulder pain or discomfort then perhaps she can implement another exercise that addresses the same muscles albeit in a pain-free fashion. In this situation, she can substitute a seated row or bent-over row for the lat pulldown. All of these exercises involve the same major muscles, namely the upper back (or "lats"), biceps and forearms.

This guideline can also be applied to aerobic and anaerobic conditioning. If an athlete cannot run due to a sprained ankle, for example, she may be able to perform aerobic and anaerobic conditioning with a non-weightbearing activity such as pedaling an upright or recumbent cycle.

## 6. Bypass the injured area.

One of the biggest advantages of machine and manual-resistance exercises is that they allow an athlete to apply the resistance above a joint so that it doesn't involve an injured area. Presume that an athlete sprained her wrist and, consequently, exercises for her torso were difficult or uncomfortable – if not impossible – to perform with conventional equipment such as barbells and dumbbells. In this case, however, she could still use machines and manual resistance to perform a variety of exercises that target the major muscles of her

Every exercise that can be performed with a barbell can also be performed with dumbbells. (Photo by Pete Silletti)

Among the machine exercises that bypass the wrist area is the pullover. (Photo by Pete Silletti)

torso without involving her wrist joint. Among the machine exercises that bypass the wrist area are the pec fly (a.k.a. the "pec dec"), pullover and lateral raise; many other exercises that avoid the wrist area can be done with manual resistance. Actually, an athlete could still perform the aforementioned exercises – and others – with machines and manual resistance even if her wrist was immobilized with a cast.

Also consider this: If an athlete's leg was immobilized such that she couldn't flex or extend her knee, it wouldn't be possible for her to perform any multiple-joint movements that address her hips such as the deadlift, leg press and hack squat. It would be possible, however, for an athlete to bypass her knee joint and train her hips in a safe and effective fashion – despite the immobilization – by doing a single-joint movement with machines or manual resistance such as hip abduction or hip adduction.

## 7. Limit the range of motion.

There's a good possibility that pain only occurs at certain points in an athlete's range of motion (ROM) such as the starting position of the repetition. In this case, she can restrict her ROM for the exercise. For example, an injury such as a hyperextended elbow or knee is especially painful in the starting (or stretched) position of a repetition. In this instance, an athlete should stop short of lowering the weight all the way down; by the same token, if pain occurs in the mid-range (or mid-point) position of a repetition, an athlete should stop short of fully flexing or extending the joint. As the injured area heals over a period of time, she can gradually and carefully increase her ROM until it's possible for her to perform repetitions that are pain-free throughout a full ROM.

Nowadays, many machines offer range-limiting devices. This enables an athlete to restrict her ROM in a precise, repeatable manner. As a matter of fact, the ROM can sometimes be adjusted in fractional increments without exiting the machine. By the way, it's a good idea to document an athlete's ROM (as well as the resistance and repetitions) that she uses during rehabilitative training.

Occasionally, an athlete's pain-free ROM may be restricted to a specific joint angle plus or minus a few degrees. Michael Bradley, the Basketball Strength and Conditioning Coach at Florida State University, sometimes prescribes an isometric (or static) contraction of varying durations to train muscles at pain-free positions. This can be accomplished by securing the lever arm of a machine such that it cannot move. After that, an athlete would exert force against this immovable resistance. Another way to do this is for an athlete to use her good limb to raise the weight to the pain-free position of her injured limb. At this point, she'd "hand off" the weight to her injured limb. Then, she'd exert force against this resistance without changing the angle of her injured limb. An athlete can also exert force isometrically against another person who's applying manual resistance. As an added measure of safety, Coach Bradley recommends a gradual build-up of force for 60 seconds in order to fatigue and weaken the muscle before maximum effort is produced. Then, he has the lifter exert maximum (pain-free) effort for an additional 30 - 60 seconds.

An athlete can implement the concept of limiting the ROM during aerobic and anaerobic conditioning. If she has knee pain while cycling, for example, she can lower the height of the seat thereby reducing the ROM of her knee joint.

## 8. Exercise the good limb.

If all else fails, an athlete can still train her unaffected limb. Here's an example: Suppose that an athlete had surgery and, as a result, her left ankle was casted. Obviously, the cast wouldn't allow her to perform any exercises that involved any ROM whatsoever for her left ankle. Even so, she could still do exercises with her right ankle.

This has important ramifications in rehabilitation because some research has shown that training a muscle on one side of the body will actually benefit the contralateral muscle (that is, the same muscle that's on the opposite side of the body). Over the years, this phenomenon has been referred to by several different names including "bilateral transfer," "cross education" and "cross transfer." Research that demonstrates a bilateral transfer of strength dates back to at least 1894 and has been confirmed in many studies since. The transfer of strength is usually small but one study reported a strength increase of 36.4% in the trained limb and a 24.7% increase in the untrained, contralateral limb. Researchers have suggested that there's a strong association between the intensity of training and the magnitude of the bilateral transfer. In other words, the greater the intensity of the exercise, the greater the degree of transfer.

Researchers aren't exactly sure why a bilateral transfer of strength occurs but one theory attributes it to neural adaptation. Support for neural adaptation comes from studies that have demonstrated increases in strength without an accompanying increase in muscular hypertrophy. It has also been theorized that the muscles that aren't being trained experience slight isometric contrac-

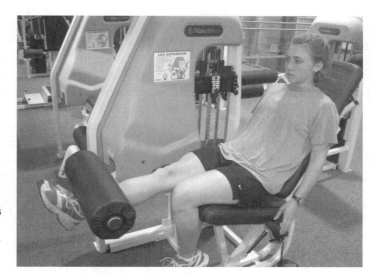

**Many exercises can be performed unilaterally – that is, with one limb at a time – on machines in a safe and comfortable fashion. (Photo by Pete Silletti)**

tions while the muscles that are being trained perform dynamic contractions through a ROM.

Regardless of why a bilateral transfer of strength occurs, the important thing to remember is that it occurs. And this neuromuscular fact can be applied to rehabilitative training. Many exercises can be performed unilaterally – that is, with one limb at a time – on machines in a safe and comfortable fashion. Indeed, numerous machines are equipped with independent movement arms that allow an athlete to train her limbs separately if needed. Basically, the independent movement arms create an independent workload. If an athlete doesn't have access to machines, she can use dumbbells and manual resistance for unilateral (single-limb) training.

Incidentally, several studies have also found that performing a skill with one limb produces an improvement in performance in the contralateral limb. This bilateral transfer of skill occurs from hand to foot as well as from hand to hand. George Sage, Ph.D., notes that the greatest bilateral transfer of skill is in the symmetrical muscle group on the opposite side of the body.

One final note of interest with respect to unilateral training: Research has also demonstrated a "bilateral deficit." Oddly enough, the force produced by two limbs contracting together is less than the sum of the forces produced by the right and left limbs contracting singly.

## 9. Exercise unaffected body parts.

In the event that an athlete cannot train an injured area due to an unreasonable amount of pain or discomfort, she can still perform exercises for her uninjured body parts. So if an athlete has a knee injury that prohibits activity for her lower body, she can still do exercises or activities for her entire torso – as long as they're done while she's sitting or lying and not standing. Likewise, if she has a shoulder injury that doesn't allow activity for the major muscles of her torso, she can still do exercises and activities for her lower body along with her arms and mid-section – provided that they don't indirectly produce shoulder pain.

Several authors have suggested an "indirect effect." Though not proven by scientific research, it's believed that exercising the larger muscles of the body will produce at least some degree of size and strength increases in other, smaller muscles even when no exercise is performed for the smaller muscles.

Once again, this guideline is also appropriate for aerobic and anaerobic conditioning. Suppose that an athlete has a hip, leg or ankle injury that prohibits her from doing any aerobic or anaerobic conditioning with her lower body. There are a few commercial devices that enable an athlete to do aerobic and anaerobic conditioning exclusively with the muscles of her torso such as an upper-body ergometer.

## PRUDENT CHOICES

In many instances, an athlete can exercise an injured area or body part in a safe, prudent and pain-free manner. This will prevent a significant loss in muscular size and strength as well as aerobic and anaerobic fitness. And even though she may not be able to exercise an injured area due to an excessive amount of pain or discomfort, she can still train her uninjured body parts. Once the injured area heals, the athlete can reintroduce exercises that were previously painful to perform.

Remember, though, that the critical factor in a prudent prescription for rehabilitative training is pain-free – or nearly pain-free – exercise and activity. That said, it's important to understand that there's a distinct difference between muscular pain and joint pain. Muscular pain isn't necessarily a cause for alarm. It's an indication that high-intensity work is being done and the muscles are being fatigued. Joint pain, however, is something else altogether. Localized pain in a joint usually means that there's some type of structural problem. If an athlete experiences pain in her joints while exercising, she's merely aggravating her condition and perhaps even causing further damage by brutalizing the joint infrastructure. Simply, an exercise that produces joint pain must be avoided or altered.

How important is rehabilitative training? According to Coach Mannie, "Our philosophy at Michigan State University has always been that strength training is a vital constituent in the rehab process and that all training options for an injured area will be considered before deciding not to address the area."

## REFERENCES

Bradley, M. 1999. Personal communication with the author (April 14).

Cannon, R. J., and E. Cafarelli. 1987. Neuromuscular adaptations to training. *Journal of Applied Physiology* 63 (6): 2396-2402.

Cook, T. W. 1933. Studies in cross-educational mirror tracing the star-shaped maze. *Journal of Experimental Psychology* 16: 144-160.

Davis, W. W. 1898. Researches in cross education. *Studies from the Yale Psychological Laboratory* 6: 6-50.

Enoka, R. M. 1988. Muscle strength and its development. *Sports Medicine* 6 (3): 146-168.

Hellebrandt, F. A. 1951. Cross education: ipsilateral and contralateral effects of unilateral training. *Journal of Applied Physiology* 4: 136-144.

Hellebrandt, F. A., A. M. Parrish and S. J. Houtz. 1947. Cross-education: the effect of unilateral exercise on the contralateral limb. *Archives of Physical Medicine and Rehabilitation* 28: 76-85.

Henry, F. M., and L. E. Smith. 1961. Simultaneous vs. separate bilateral muscular contractions in relation to neural overflow theory and neuromotor specificity. *Research Quarterly* 32: 42-46.

Housh, D. J., T. J. Housh, J. P. Weir, L. L. Weir, P. E. Donlin and W. K. Chu. 1996. Concentric isokinetic training and hypertrophy of the quadriceps femoris muscle. *Medicine and Science in Sports and Exercise* 28 (5): 684.

Ikai, M., and T. Fukunaga. 1970. A study on training effect on strength per unit cross-sectional area of human muscle by means of ultrasonic measurement. *Internationale Zeitschrift fur angewandte Physiologie einschliessich Arbeitphysiologie* 28: 173-180.

Jones, A., M. L. Pollock, J. E. Graves, M. Fulton, W. Jones, M. MacMillan, D. D. Baldwin and J. Cirulli. 1988. *Safe, specific testing and rehabilitative exercise of the muscles of the lumbar spine.* Santa Barbara, CA: Sequoia Communications.

Komi, P. V., J. H. T. Viitasalo, R. Rauramaa and V. Vihko. 1978. Effect of isometric strength training on mechanical, electrical and metabolic aspects of muscle function. *European Journal of Applied Physiology* 40 (1): 45-55.

Krotkiewski, M., A. Aniansson, G. Grimby, P. Bjorntarp and L. Sjostrom. 1979. The effect of unilateral isokinetic strength training on local adipose and muscle tissue morphology, thickness and enzymes. *European Journal of Physiology* 42 (4): 271-281.

Lambrinides, T. 1989. Indirect transfer of strength. *High Intensity Training Newsletter* 1 (4): 5-6.

Mathews, D. K., C. T. Shay, F. Godin and R. Hogdon. 1956. Cross transfer effects of training on strength and endurance. *Research Quarterly* 27: 206-212.

Mannie, K. 1999. Personal communication with the author (April 15).

Moritani, T., and H. A. deVries. 1979. Neural factors vs hypertrophy in the course of muscle strength gain. *American Journal of Physical Medicine and Rehabilitation* 58 (3): 115-130.

Munn, N. L. 1953. Bilateral transfer of learning. *Journal of Experimental Psychology* 15: 343-353.

Ohtsuki, T. 1981. Decrease in grip strength induced by simultaneous bilateral exertion with reference to finger strength. *Ergonomics* 24 (1): 37-48.

Rasch, P. J., and C. E. Morehouse. 1957. Effect of static and dynamic exercises on muscular strength and hypertrophy. *Journal of Applied Physiology* 11 (1): 29-34.

Sage, G. H. 1977. *Introduction to motor behavior: a neuropsychological approach. 2d ed*. Reading, MA: Addison-Wesley Publishing Company.

Scripture, E. W., T. L. Smith and E. M. Brown. 1894. On the education of muscular control and power. *Studies from the Yale Psychological Laboratory* 2: 114-119.

Slater-Hammel, A. T. 1950. Bilateral effects of muscle activity. *Research Quarterly* 21: 203-209.

Swift, E. J. 1903. Studies in the psychology and physiology of learning. *American Journal of Psychology* 14: 201-251.

Vandervoort, A. A., D. G. Sale and J. R. Moroz. 1987. Strength-velocity relationship and fatiguability of unilateral versus bilateral arm extension. *European Journal of Applied Physiology* 56 (2): 201-205.

Yasuda, Y., and M. Miyamura. 1983. Cross-transfer effects of muscular training on blood flow in the ipsilateral and contralateral forearms. *European Journal of Applied Physiology* 51 (3): 321-329.

# 9

# The Fundamentals of Sports Conditioning

*Tom Kelso, M.S., S.C.C.C., C.S.C.S.*

In order to excel in sports, athletes must be as highly conditioned as possible. There are several benefits of engaging in sports conditioning. For example, a sound program of sports conditioning . . .

- delays the onset of fatigue to prolong maximum performance potential by improving cardiorespiratory endurance and the ability to recover from repetitive maximal efforts over the course of competition
- adapts to the movement demands that are encountered during competition such as straight-line sprinting, backward/lateral running and other change-of-direction/movement situations
- protects against injury due to the development of a more functional and durable body that can better withstand forces and potentially dangerous situations in competition and practices
- assists in caloric expenditure to facilitate either a negative, steady-state or positive caloric balance for those on a program for weight (fat) loss, weight maintenance or weight (muscle) gain

In order to be effective and productive, sports conditioning must adhere to a number of guidelines. The following are key points for athletes and coaches:

- Train the way you perform. Utilize sport-related movement drills and efforts that maximize the energy system(s) that are needed for optimal performance.
- Use a variety of training methods. Long and short intervals, shuttle runs, sprints, agility drills and other change-of-direction drills can all improve conditioning while simultaneously adding variety to training.
- Understand that conditioning methods overlap. Cardiorespiratory endurance can be developed in a number of ways including the use of short sprints and functional speed/agility drills. Likewise, speed can be enhanced by not only using sport-related drills but also through improved cardiorespiratory endurance which helps sustain maximum speed efforts.
- Be progressive. As an athlete adapts to various training stimuli, she must be exposed to greater workloads for further adaptations in cardiorespiratory endurance and other running abilities.
- Work at an appropriate intensity level. To develop maximum speed, agility

and endurance, training must be done at a specific intensity level for that specific mode of training. Simply stated, to get better at sprinting, an athlete must run at full-speed. To develop endurance, an athlete must run at a level that elevates and maintains her heart rate. To improve agility and change-of-direction ability, an athlete must perform drills using the maximum speed that allows for the proper performance of such drills.

- Balance the conditioning program with strength training. Both strength training and conditioning are important for total development. Possessing great strength alone will not optimally prepare an athlete for competition. Likewise, possessing good cardiorespiratory endurance but having weak muscles isn't a viable option. However, both require time and energy to complete. Attempt to improve both conditioning and strength levels in the most logical manner.

- Allow for sufficient recovery. Proper rest and nutrition are vital to recover properly from training sessions and progress in development. Adequate recovery time and proper nutritional intake must be provided if the body is to adapt to training demands and improve fitness levels.

## FATIGUE

Muscular fatigue is the primary reason why a conditioning program is necessary. Ultimately, overtaxing the body – or a specific energy system – eventually leads to fatigue and diminished performance.

Fatigue can be a very complex issue. Generally, fatigue can result from one or more of the following causes (Bouchard et al. 1990; Wilmore and Costill 1988):

- a decrease in phosphocreatine
- a decrease in glycogen

It's important to balance the conditioning program with strength training. (Photo by Pete Silletti)

- a reduction in blood-glucose levels
- an increased accumulation of waste products
- an alteration of the physiochemical properties of muscle
- a disturbance in the function of the nervous system
- a change in the concentration of the ratio of free tryptophan to branch chain amino acids in the bloodstream
- an environmental stress on the homeostasis of the body (such as dehydration) that results in heat exhaustion/stroke

A goal, then, of any conditioning program is to minimize fatigue – or, at best, delay the onset of it – to help maximize performance potential. To better understand the dilemma of fatigue and its specific underlying issues, a closer look at the energy systems is required.

## AN OVERVIEW OF THE ENERGY SYSTEMS

Muscle contraction is fueled by adenosine triphosphate (ATP). As the name suggests, ATP consists of an adenosine component bonded to three phosphate groups. When a bond is broken, energy is released which ultimately catalyzes muscle-fiber activation and consequent sport-skill movement/actions (Wilmore and Costill 1988).

The body has a limited amount of ATP. In order to continue doing physical work, ATP must be rebuilt. During any activity there are three primary means of rebuilding ATP for muscle contraction: two anaerobic processes and an aerobic process. The anaerobic processes rebuild ATP without oxygen; the aerobic process rebuilds ATP with oxygen.

The two anaerobic processes are the ATP-PC System and the Lactic Acid System. The aerobic process – the Aerobic System – can be considered a system in itself. The efforts of these three energy systems rebuild ATP. Their contribution to work output depends upon the total capacity of the system, the rate of ATP use and the intensity of the activity (Dudley and Murray 1982).

Although all three energy systems basically "turn on" at the onset of any activity, it's primarily the length and intensity of the activity that dictates which system is more predominant in supplying ATP (Dudley and Murray 1982).

### The ATP-PC System

The ATP-PC system can be considered the high-intensity/short-duration supplier of energy. It's used predominantly in short burst or short sprint-type activities. Phosphagens (immediate stores of ATP) and the resynthesis of phosphocreatine (PC) to rebuild ATP all provide the energy for muscle contraction. This system is very powerful but can only provide ATP for a limited time during maximal activity (Jones, McCartney and McComas 1986).

## ATP-PC fatigue

The immediate stores of ATP and the resynthesis of phosphocreatine to rebuild ATP are very limited. The capacity of this system is confined to a maximum of approximately 12 seconds during high-intensity work (McFarlane 1983).

When totally depleted, restoration of the ATP-PC System occurs during a recovery period. The time needed to replenish the system is summarized in Table 9.1 (Murray 1980).

To better understand this, assume a maximum-speed, 12-second sprint was used to exhaust the ATP-PC System. After a recovery period of approximately 20 seconds, 50% of its capacity would then be restored and available to generate ATP. Note, however, that it would take approximately five minutes or more to restore the system to its full capacity. This is the rationale as to why maximum-speed sprint efforts can only be repeated after lengthy periods or recovery.

## The Lactic Acid System

The Lactic Acid (LA) System is basically a medium-intensity/medium-duration supplier of energy. ATP is rebuilt through the process of glycolysis – literally, the breakdown of glycogen – to provide energy in longer sprints or activities of the same nature. The LA System has only 50% of the power of the ATP-PC System but twice its capacity (Dudley and Murray 1982).

## Lactic acid fatigue

The breakdown of glycogen to rebuild ATP provides muscle energy in sub-maximal but intense activities ranging from approximately 30 seconds to a little more than one minute or in extended activities that consist of periodic high-intensity efforts (McFarlane 1983).

Glycolysis also produces lactic acid. The "lactate threshold" is the point where lactic acid begins to accumulate. As the acidity of the muscle increases, the presence of protons (hydrogen ions) from lactic-acid accumulation eventually interferes with muscle contraction. The ability of chemicals in the muscles and bloodstream to absorb or "buffer" the protons allows for the activity to continue. The inability to buffer protons eventually shuts down the system. This explains the burning sensation that's often felt in the muscles at the point of fatigue during a very intense activity.

The key to buffering the protons is transporting them to the bloodstream. Compared to muscles, the blood has a greater capacity to buffer protons. The heavy breathing that follows intense exercise serves this purpose. This heavy breathing – called "oxygen debt" – increases the amount of oxygen being consumed and does two things. First, it increases the blood flow through the muscles, pushing the protons into the bloodstream where the majority of them are broken down and eventually released through expiration. Second, it pays the "debt" that's "owed" from using the anaerobic systems as it rebuilds ATP (Bouchard et al. 1990).

| ELAPSED TIME (min: sec) | AMOUNT REPLENISHED |
|---|---|
| 0:20 | 50% |
| 0:40 | 75% |
| 1:00 | 87% |
| 2:00 | 93% |
| 5:00+ | 100% |

**TABLE 9.1: TIME NEEDED TO REPLENISH THE ATP-PC SYSTEM**

| ELAPSED TIME (hr: min) | AMOUNT REPLENISHED |
|---|---|
| 0:25 | 50% |
| 0:50 | 75% |
| 1:15 | 87% |
| 2:00 | 100% |

**TABLE 9.2: TIME NEEDED TO REPLENISH THE LACTIC ACID SYSTEM**

In restoring the LA System, approximately 60% of the lactic acid is aerobically metabolized, 20% is converted to glucose and 15% is converted to protein. The remaining 5% is eventually perspired or urinated from the body.

The restoration process of the LA System is lengthier than the ATP-PC System. The timeline for restoration of the LA System is summarized in Table 9.2 (Fleck and Kraemer 1987).

## The Aerobic System

The Aerobic System is the low-intensity/long-duration supplier of energy. ATP is rebuilt through the breakdown of foodstuff with oxygen – essentially, the process of aerobic metabolism – and provides the energy for lengthy activities such as distance running or general low-level work throughout the day. The Aerobic System is the least powerful of the three but has the greatest capacity to perform work (Dudley and Murray 1982).

## Aerobic fatigue

Aerobic restoration of ATP through the oxidation of foodstuff has a very large capacity for low-level, long-term work. Protein, fat and carbohydrates can all be converted to energy but it's fat that's most efficiently metabolized in aerobic work. In fact, fat has an almost unlimited potential to supply energy. The ultimate cause of fatigue even in aerobic-type exercise, therefore, is the total depletion of glycogen. This occurs only in cases of very extended but intense activities such as running a marathon and competing in a triathlon (Bouchard et al. 1990).

Compared to the two anaerobic systems, restoration of the Aerobic System is a different picture. Although glycogen is always a limiting factor, it's

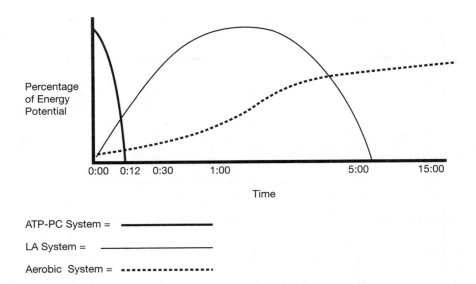

ATP-PC System = ────────────

LA System = ────────────

Aerobic System = ••••••••••••••••••

continually restoring itself through the periodic consumption of foodstuff and the availability of virtually an unlimited supply of fat. Only in extreme cases does it become significantly depleted. For the most part, some form of food-stuff is available for continued functioning of the Aerobic System.

## THE ENERGY CONTINUUM

The relationship and potential of all three energy systems can be better understood by examining Figure 9.1. Again, it's important to know that all three systems are triggered at the onset of any activity. The length and intensity of the activity dictates what system is taxed the greatest (Dudley and Murray 1982). This relationship is illustrated in Figure 9.1.

The energy systems work in harmony to furnish ATP for the working muscles. As the Aerobic System constantly supplies oxygen to the muscles, the two anaerobic systems function to support higher levels of work that may be encountered. The harsh reality is that each system does have its own limitation with the two anaerobic systems being more limited than the Aerobic System.

It's also important to understand the overlap of the three systems. Many activities are dependent upon the use of all energy systems at some point which requires a transition from one system to another. Much of this is contingent upon which system is taxed the heaviest at the time. As one system begins to decline – and if the activity level is to be maintained – another system is called upon to continue the activity.

A perfect example of this is running. When starting a run at a very slow pace, the Aerobic System (low level) is the primary source of fuel. If the running pace is increased to a full sprint, the ATP-PC System is then heavily taxed. A full sprint cannot be maintained for a long period – due to ATP-PC fatigue – so running speed naturally must decrease to something less than an all-out sprint (such as to a 3/4-speed stride) and then is fueled by the LA System. Finally, as this running pace continues, the speed eventually declines as a result of glycogen depletion and, hence, the fatigue of the LA System. The heavy breathing that occurs at this point indicates that both anaerobic systems were heavily taxed but the slow pace can still be continued via the Aerobic System. So the Aerobic System supported the athlete's efforts across the entire spectrum from slow-paced running to full-speed sprinting and back to slow-paced running. In other words, from dependence upon the Aerobic System → ATP-PC System → LA System → back to the Aerobic System (as anaerobic fatigue eventually sets in and slows the entire endeavor).

The overlap and transition between the three energy systems are summarized in Table 9.3 (Edington and Edgerton 1976).

| TIME INTERVAL(min:sec) | PRIMARY SYSTEM USED |
|---|---|
| 0:00 - 0:02 | immediate ATP stores |
| 0:02 - 0:12 | ATP-PC System |
| 0:12 - 0:30 | transition from ATP-PC System to LA System |
| 0:30 - 1:30 | LA System (glycolosis) |
| 1:30 - 5:00 | transition from LA System to Aerobic System |
| 5:00 or more | Aerobic System |

TABLE 9.3: OVERLAP AND TRANSITION BETWEEN THE THREE ENERGY SYSTEMS

## Overall Cardiorespiratory Conditioning

The importance of overall cardiorespiratory development shouldn't be overlooked. Indeed, it's vital for most sports. Over the course of a competition, repeated speed and power actions can eventually result in fatigue and, thus, decreased performance. Therefore, an athlete must be able to recover adequately between each speed and power bout in order to continually perform at her maximum potential. Although most athletic events primarily require anaerobic speed and power actions, longer-duration interval and aerobic work should be performed to develop the endurance that's needed to support and enhance all short-term speed and power activities. Sprints and short-burst power training by themselves may not be enough to adequately develop overall endurance. As such, long interval-type training can be of value for total cardiorespiratory development and support of the anaerobic energy systems.

Regardless of the overlap of the energy systems, it's obvious that the Aerobic System is important to both of the anaerobic systems. Not only does it allow for the "repayment" of anaerobic work, a good aerobic capacity enhances the entire cardiorespiratory system in the following ways (Bouchard et al. 1990):

1. delivering nutrients to the cells as well and eliminating waste products from the cells

2. cooling the body during any exercise/activity – especially from the effects of environmental heat

3. controlling the degree of muscle acidity

4. offering resistance to disease organisms

Understanding the energy systems and how they function relative to training intensity and recovery time is critical. An athlete can train smarter with greater purpose and have a better appreciation for a sports-conditioning program.

## THE BASICS

For an athlete to achieve optimal results, sports conditioning must adhere to certain principles. A sports-conditioning program can be established by following these basic guidelines:

1. Incorporate a logical plan based upon the principles of overload, recovery/adaptation and progression.

2. Schedule it in conjunction with other energy-utilizing training components and physical activities (such as strength training and practice sessions).

3. Base it upon the specific energy system(s)/sport demand needs.

4. Use a variety of training methods for total development (if possible).

5. Conduct the program in an organized manner that includes a pre-workout warm-up routine, organized running groups and a post-workout cool-down period.

## OVERLOAD/PROPER TRAINING INTENSITY

To obtain maximum benefits, the principles of overload, recovery/adaptation and progression should govern a conditioning program. In brief, this involves three guidelines:

1. Place a demand on the body or system.

2. Allow time to recover from and adapt to this demand.

3. Apply greater workloads as conditioning levels improve for further enhancements.

First and foremost is the overload demand. To overload the ATP-PC, LA and Aerobic Systems, a level of training intensity that taxes the particular pathway needs to be generated relative to the duration (distance/length) of the bout. Proper training intensity can simply be obtained by altering the running/movement speed (again, relative to the duration component). In general, targeting the ATP-PC and/or LA Systems involve shorter efforts or drills with relatively faster running speeds (and higher potential training heart rates). The LA and/or Aerobic Systems involve longer efforts or drills with relatively slower running speeds (and lower potential training heart rates, all other factors being equal).

To further facilitate an overload of the energy systems, three training variables – frequency, intensity and recovery – can be manipulated relative to the duration component. At this point, it's necessary to define several terms. "Frequency" is the volume or number of efforts/drills; "intensity" is the speed of each effort/drill; "recovery" is the interval between efforts/drills (if applicable). When an athlete can perform a number of efforts/bouts at an increased level of intensity with minimal recovery between them, her level of conditioning has, naturally, improved. This is the ultimate goal of the sports-conditioning program: to improve maximal work output potential over the course of an entire athletic contest.

## Determining Appropriate Heart Rates

The heart rate during and following an exercise or other physical activity is a reasonable means by which to monitor training intensity and target energy systems. There are several different heart rates that must be considered including the resting heart rate (RHR), maximum heart rate (MHR) and training heart rate (THR).

The RHR can be determined by taking the pulse at either the wrist (just above the thumb) or the neck (the right or left side). To get the number of beats per minute (bpm), count the beats in a 10-second period and multiply by six.

The MHR can be calculated by subtracting age from 220. For example, the MHR of a 21-year-old individual would be 199 bpm [220 - 21 = 199]. The MHR is important for calculating an optimal THR for anaerobic and aerobic training as well as proper recovery times.

The THR should be at or more than about 85% of the MHR for maximum anaerobic benefits; the THR should be about 70 - 80% of the MHR for maximum aerobic benefits. Using a MHR of 199 bpm, the THR for anaerobic training should be at least 169 bpm [199 x 0.85 = 169]; the THR for aerobic training should be about 139 - 159 bpm [199 x 0.70 = 139; 199 x 0.80 = 159].

When using the heart-rate recovery method during anaerobic training, the pulse should drop to about 120 - 140 bpm, depending upon the energy system that's targeted (ATP-PC or LA).

## Overloading the ATP-PC System

In order to effectively overload the ATP-PC System, the following training variables must be considered:

- frequency – perform multiple bouts of exercises/drills. For instance, an athlete would complete approximately 10 - 20+ repetitions/efforts.
- duration – do up to about 12 seconds (0:12) of maximum effort.
- intensity – use a maximum, high-level effort with a THR of about 85% or more of maximum. Note that the THR may not reach that level when performing very brief bouts (such as 1 - 4 seconds).
- recovery (by time) – take a recovery period that's as much as 10 times or more the actual work period. For instance, a sprint that takes 0:10 (10 sec-

onds) would get about 1:40 of recovery (a ratio of 10:1); a sprint that takes 0:06 would get about 1:30 of recovery (a ratio of 15:1).

- recovery (by heart rate) – take a recovery period such that the RHR drops to about 120 bpm.

Here are several specific examples of how an athlete can overload her ATP-PC System:

- Sprint Training – run 10 40-yard sprints (10 x 40 yd), each one at full speed, with a recovery of 1:20 between each sprint (or when the RHR drops to about 120 bpm).
- Functional Speed and Agility (FSA) Training – do Reaction and Quickness (RAQ) Drills consisting of three patterns repeated four times (3 x 4) with a full recovery between each effort (or when the RHR drops to about 120 bpm); do Change-of-Direction (COD) Drills consisting of three patterns repeated four times (3 x 4) with at least 1:00 of recovery between each effort (or when the RHR drops to about 120 bpm).
- Position-Specific Drills (PSD) – perform various patterns and repetitions of maximum-effort Position-Specific Drills done with a full recovery between each effort (or when the RHR drops to about 120 bpm).

## Overloading the LA System

In order to effectively overload the LA System, the following training variables must be considered:

- frequency – perform multiple bouts of exercises/drills. For instance, an athlete would complete approximately 3 - 20 repetitions/efforts.
- duration – do about 0:12 - 0:30 (the approximate transition from the ATP-PC to the LA System) and/or about 0:30 - 1:30 (the "normal" LA System) of effort.
- intensity – use a moderately high to high level of effort with a THR of about 85% or more of maximum.
- recovery (by time): take a recovery period of about 0.5 - 4.5 times the actual work period. For instance, a sprint that takes 1:00 would get about 2:30 of recovery (a ratio of 2.5:1); a sprint that takes 0:25 would get about 1:20 of recovery (a ratio of 3.25:1).
- recovery (by heart rate): take a recovery period such that the RHR drops to about 120 - 140 bpm.

Here are several specific examples of how an athlete can overload her LA System:

- Interval Training – do five 400-yard runs (5 x 400 yd), each one in 1:07 with a recovery of 3:20 between each run (or when the RHR drops to about 120 - 140 bpm).

- Interval Training – run eight 200-yard shuttles (8 x 200 yd) each one in 0:40, with a recovery of 2:20 between each shuttle (or when the RHR drops to about 120 - 140 bpm).

- Metabolic Agility Stations – do six stations of 5:00 each with a recovery of 1:15 between each station (or when the RHR drops to about 120 - 140 bpm).

With interval training, manipulating one training variable – with the others remaining constant – can lead to a greater overload of the LA System and, eventually, improved fitness. A sample six-week period of training that depicts this is given in Figure 9.2.

| VARIABLE | WEEK 1 | WEEK 6 | CONSTANTS |
|----------|--------|--------|-----------|
| Frequency | 6 x 200 yd<br>@ 0:36<br>1:48 recovery | 12 x 200 yd<br>@ 0:36<br>1:48 recovery | duration<br>intensity<br>recovery |
| Duration | 6 x 200 yd<br>@ 0:36<br>1:48 recovery | 6 x 200 m (218 yd)<br>@ 0:36<br>1:48 recovery | frequency<br>intensity<br>recovery |
| Intensity | 6 x 200 yd<br>@ 0:36<br>1:48 recovery | 6 x 200 yd<br>@ 0:32<br>1:48 recovery | frequency/duration<br><br>recovery |
| Recovery | 6 x 200 yd<br>@ 0:36<br>1:48 recovery | 6 x 200 yd<br>@ 0:36<br>1:30 recovery | frequency/duration<br><br>intensity |

FIGURE 9.2: EXAMPLE OF MANIPULATING VARIABLES DURING INTERVAL TRAINING

## Overloading the Aerobic System

In order to effectively overload the Aerobic System, the following training variables must be considered:

- frequency – perform single, steady-state bouts (such as continuous, long-distance or fartlek training) or multiple bouts (such as aerobic intervals). For instance, an athlete would run continuously for 1.5+ miles (continuous or fartlek training) or complete approximately 6 - 30+ repetitions/efforts (aerobic intervals).

- duration – do about 1:30 - 5:00 (the approximate transition from the LA to the Aerobic System) and/or about 5:00 or more (the "normal" Aerobic System) of effort.

- intensity – use a low to moderate level of effort with a THR of about 70 - 80% of maximum.

- recovery (by time) – for aerobic intervals, take a recovery period of about 0.4 - 1.0 times the actual work period. For instance, an effort that takes 3:00 would get about 1:12 of recovery (a ratio of 0.4:1); an effort that takes 0:30 would get about 0:30 of recovery (a ratio of 1:1).

- recovery (by heart rate) – for aerobic intervals, take a recovery period such that the RHR reaches no lower than about 140 bpm.

Here are several specific examples of how an athlete can overload her Aerobic System:

- Long Aerobic Intervals – do six 600-meter runs (6 x 600 m), each one in 3:00 with a recovery of 1:12 between each run (or when the RHR reaches no lower than about 140 bpm).
- Short Aerobic Intervals – do 30 100-yard runs (30 x 100 yd), each one in 0:27 with a recovery of 0:27 between each run (or when the RHR reaches no lower than about 140 bpm).
- Fartlek Training – run 12 laps around the perimeter of a football field in a time of 22:00, alternating between walking, jogging and sprinting at random intervals.

## RECOVERY/ADAPTATION: A LOGICAL PLAN OF TRAINING

Adequate recovery time between training sessions is paramount in order to (1) recover from the overload stresses incurred in individual training sessions and (2) adapt to these stresses and actually improve the level of conditioning to attain greater ability. Therefore, the training exposures must be scheduled logically – especially when an athlete is also recovering from the demands of other activities such as strength training and sport practice sessions. Because of this, a proper balance of all training components is critical and a systematic plan of training should be implemented for optimal adaptation/preparation.

Any type of productive training requires energy and leaves the body in a depleted state. This must be accounted for when scheduling the various training components. Therefore, when combining strength training, conditioning and sport practice sessions, consideration must be given to session readiness. That is, an athlete should go into each session having recovered as much as possible from the previous session(s). Quite often, this is impossible as time is limited and taking full days of recovery becomes impractical. Nevertheless, energy-depleting sessions can be scheduled logically if certain guidelines are followed for out-of-season and in-season training.

These are several suggestions for out-of-season training:

- Avoid scheduling high-level conditioning sessions (such as short intervals, sprints or agility-type drills) and lower-body strength training on the same day.
- Avoid similar high-level conditioning the day following any lower-body strength training (if possible).
- Do conditioning on upper-body strength-training days (if following a split-type strength-training routine).

- Do conditioning the day before lower-body strength training (if possible).
- Include a full day of recovery (no activity) somewhere in the week – especially following two consecutive training days (if possible).

Based upon these suggestions, eight different formats for out-of-season training are given in Figures 9.3 - 9.10. The formats include five- and seven-day plans that can incorporate either total-body or split-body strength training.

| SUNDAY | MONDAY | TUESDAY | WEDNESDAY | THURSDAY | FRIDAY | SATURDAY |
|---|---|---|---|---|---|---|
| | Conditioning | Strength Training Total Body | Recovery | Conditioning | Strength Training Total Body | |

**FIGURE 9.3: FIVE-DAY PLAN WITH TWO TOTAL-BODY WORKOUTS**

| SUNDAY | MONDAY | TUESDAY | WEDNESDAY | THURSDAY | FRIDAY | SATURDAY |
|---|---|---|---|---|---|---|
| | Conditioning | Strength Training Total Body | Recovery | Strength Training Upper Body Conditioning | Strength Training Lower Body | |

**FIGURE 9.4: FIVE-DAY PLAN WITH TOTAL-BODY AND SPLIT-BODY STRENGTH TRAINING**

| SUNDAY | MONDAY | TUESDAY | WEDNESDAY | THURSDAY | FRIDAY | SATURDAY |
|---|---|---|---|---|---|---|
| | Strength Training Upper Body Conditioning | Strength Training Lower Body | Recovery | Strength Training Upper Body Conditioning | Strength Training Lower Body | |

**FIGURE 9.5: FIVE-DAY PLAN WITH SPLIT-BODY STRENGTH TRAINING**

| SUNDAY | MONDAY | TUESDAY | WEDNESDAY | THURSDAY | FRIDAY | SATURDAY |
|---|---|---|---|---|---|---|
| | Strength Training Upper Body Conditioning | Recovery | Strength Training Lower Body | Recovery | Strength Training Upper Body Conditioning | |
| | Strength Training Lower Body | Recovery | Strength Training Upper Body Conditioning | Recovery | Strength Training Lower Body | |

**FIGURE 9.6: TWO-WEEK ROTATION, FIVE-DAY PLAN WITH SPLIT-BODY STRENGTH TRAINING**

| SUNDAY | MONDAY | TUESDAY | WEDNESDAY | THURSDAY | FRIDAY | SATURDAY |
|---|---|---|---|---|---|---|
| Strength Training Total Body | | Conditioning | Strength Training Total Body | | Conditioning | Strength Training Total Body |
| | Conditioning | Strength Training Total Body | | Conditioning | Strength Training Total Body | |
| Conditioning | Strength Training Total Body | | Conditioning | Strength Training Total Body | | Conditioning |

**FIGURE 9.7: THREE-WEEK ROTATION, SEVEN-DAY PLAN WITH TOTAL-BODY STRENGTH TRAINING**

| SUNDAY | MONDAY | TUESDAY | WEDNESDAY | THURSDAY | FRIDAY | SATURDAY |
|---|---|---|---|---|---|---|
| Strength Training Upper Body / Conditioning | Strength Training Lower Body | | Strength Training Upper Body / Conditioning | Strength Training Lower Body | | Strength Training Upper Body / Conditioning |
| Strength Training Lower Body | | Strength Training Upper Body / Conditioning | Strength Training Lower Body | | Strength Training Upper Body / Conditioning | Strength Training Lower Body |
| | Strength Training Upper Body / Conditioning | Strength Training Lower Body | | Strength Training Upper Body / Conditioning | Strength Training Lower Body | |

**FIGURE 9.8: THREE-WEEK ROTATION, SEVEN-DAY PLAN WITH SPLIT-BODY STRENGTH TRAINING**

| SUNDAY | MONDAY | TUESDAY | WEDNESDAY | THURSDAY | FRIDAY | SATURDAY |
|---|---|---|---|---|---|---|
| Strength Training Upper Body Conditioning | | Strength Training Lower Body | | Strength Training Upper Body Conditioning | | Strength Training Lower Body |
| | Strength Training Upper Body Conditioning | | Strength Training Lower Body | | Strength Training Upper Body Conditioning | |
| Strength Training Lower Body | | Strength Training Upper Body Conditioning | | Strength Training Lower Body | | Strength Training Upper Body Conditioning |
| | Strength Training Lower Body | | Strength Training Upper Body Conditioning | | Strength Training Lower Body | |

**FIGURE 9.9: FOUR-WEEK ROTATION, SEVEN-DAY PLAN WITH SPLIT-BODY STRENGTH TRAINING**

| SUNDAY | MONDAY | TUESDAY | WEDNESDAY | THURSDAY | FRIDAY | SATURDAY |
|---|---|---|---|---|---|---|
| Strength Training Total Body | | Conditioning | | Strength Training Total Body | | Conditioning |
| | Strength Training Total Body | | Conditioning | | Strength Training Total Body | |
| Conditioning | | Strength Training Total Body | | Conditioning | | Strength Training Total Body |
| | Conditioning | | Strength Training Total Body | | Conditioning | |

**FIGURE 9.10: FOUR-WEEK ROTATION, SEVEN-DAY PLAN WITH TOTAL-BODY STRENGTH TRAINING**

These are several suggestions for in-season training:

- Do training (conditioning or strength training) after the practice sessions if sport-skill practice and training must be done back-to-back on the same day.
- Conduct training far-removed from practice sessions (such as in the morning at least six hours prior to practice) if sport-skill practice and training must be done on the same day and the training component cannot be done following practice.
- Perform any in-season conditioning at least 48 hours prior to competition to assure adequate recovery. (*Note*: Weekly formats for in-season conditioning are addressed later in this chapter.)

## PROGRESSIVE TRAINING

Once the body has fully recovered, adapted and improved in fitness levels as a result of training overloads, it can tolerate more work and/or demonstrate greater ability. Therefore, as conditioning levels improve, workout overloads must be progressively greater for further improvement in endurance, speed and agility. To gain the most out of the program, progression should occur within the individual workout variables as well as the modes of training.

## PROGRESSION OF INDIVIDUAL WORKOUT VARIABLES

In conditioning, progressive overload is governed by the previously discussed training variables of frequency (the number of drills/efforts), duration (the length/time of each), intensity (the performance speed/effort exuded) and recovery (the time between drills/efforts, if applicable). Manipulating these variables over time for the sake of progressive training must be done systematically.

There are numerous ways by which to make training progressive. The primary focus should be to simply do more over time in terms of work output. Stated otherwise, it's being able to work at a higher level for a longer period of time – the essence of being "in shape."

In the initial stages of a conditioning program – the first weeks of an out-of-season program – athletes begin with low-level training and gradually progress to higher levels based upon the volume, intensity and work:rest ratio.

In general, the approach would look something like this:

## Low-level workouts

- volume – a lower number of efforts/bouts (relative to the length/distance)
- intensity – a lower level of effort
- work:rest ratio – a higher recovery period between efforts/bouts

## Moderate-level workouts

- volume – a moderate number of efforts/bouts (relative to the length/distance)

- intensity – a moderate level of effort
- work:rest ratio – a moderate recovery period between efforts/bouts

## High-level workouts

- volume – a higher number of efforts/bouts (relative to the length/distance)
- intensity – a higher level of effort
- work:rest ratio – a lower recovery period between efforts/bouts

## MODE OF TRAINING PROGRESSION

Over the course of training periods, progression shouldn't only occur in terms of the aforementioned training variables but also with the modes of train-

| SUNDAY | MONDAY | TUESDAY | WEDNESDAY | THURSDAY | FRIDAY | SATURDAY |
|---|---|---|---|---|---|---|
| Strength Training Total Body | | Long Intervals Low Level | Strength Training Total Body | | Long Intervals Low Level | Strength Training Total Body |
| | Long Intervals Low Level | Strength Training Total Body | | Long Intervals Low Level | Strength Training Total Body | |
| Long Intervals Moderate Level | Strength Training Total Body | | Long Intervals Moderate Level | Strength Training Total Body | | Short Intervals Low Level |
| Strength Training Total Body | | Short Intervals Low Level | Strength Training Total Body | | Short Intervals Moderate Level | Strength Training Total Body |
| | Short Intervals Moderate Level | Strength Training Total Body | | COD & Short Sprints Low Level | Strength Training Total Body | |
| Short Intervals Moderate Level | Strength Training Total Body | | COD & Short Sprints Low Level | Strength Training Total Body | | Short Intervals High Level |
| Strength Training Total Body | | COD & Short Sprints Moderate Level | Strength Training Total Body | | Short Intervals High Level | Strength Training Total Body |
| | RAQ, PSD & Short Sprints Moderate Level | Strength Training Total Body | | PSD & COD High Level | Strength Training Total Body | |
| RAQ, PSD & Shuttle Runs High Level | Strength Training Total Body | | PSD, COD & Short Sprints Moderate Level | Strength Training Total Body | | RAQ, PSD & COD High Level |
| Strength Training Total Body | | RAQ, PSD & Shuttle Runs High Level | Strength Training Total Body | | RAQ, PSD & Short Sprints High Level | Strength Training Total Body |

**FIGURE 9.11: TEN-WEEK PERIOD, THREE-WEEK ROTATION ON A SEVEN-DAY PLAN WITH TOTAL-BODY STRENGTH TRAINING**

ing relative to a specific sport and its demands. One proven, systematic plan is the "long-to-short" progression. This entails the use of longer, less intense, general efforts/drills in the initial weeks of a training period and tapering down to shorter, more intense, sport-related efforts/drills in the latter weeks prior to the competitive season. Lower-intensity efforts allow an athlete to progressively adapt to training overloads while still targeting her cardiorespiratory endurance. Over time, the intensity level picks up and more intense efforts/drills are incorporated that better parallel the energy/movement demands of competition.

An example of a 10-week, out-of-season program is shown in Figure 9.11. This application shows how to schedule various modes of conditioning and total-body strength training.

## SPORT-RELATED CONDITIONING

Although true specificity of training entails exact practice of the skills/techniques that are required in competition, sport-related activities have a place in a conditioning program. Sport-related conditioning should be performed to (1) tax and improve upon the energy systems that are required for optimal performance and (2) expose the body to the demands of actual competition.

Sport-related cardiorespiratory fitness should also be developed to enhance endurance to delay the onset of fatigue. This can be done using drills or general conditioning methods that target the primary energy system(s) but which are independent of the exact sport skills that are used in the sport (such as long interval or fartlek training).

### Skill Training: Specific and Exact

To become better at a specific skill, an athlete needs to practice the actual skill. To become better at blocking a volleyball, breaking for a ground ball or jumping for a rebound, she must practice these exact skills. Likewise, other game/contest situations – such as plays, maneuvers and contingencies – should be drilled repeatedly in practice to improve them. Athletes must be exposed to the exactness of competition – the details and intricacies of specific sport skills and situations – in order play at their optimal levels.

### Justifying Sport-Related Conditioning

In conditioning, there are some drills that can be performed which may not be exactly specific to athletic skills and/or contest situations but, to an extent, replicate similar in-sport energy demands and, thus, serve an "adaptive" purpose. For example, backpedaling, stopping, changing directions and moving quickly in another direction can be incorporated into a sports-conditioning program to adapt to this demand (although it may not be done this exact way in competition). The bottom line: When training the energy systems, get as close to the skill as possible.

There are several other reasons to include sport-related conditioning. First, an athlete will be able to recover from repetitive, short-term, energy-depleting skill executions during a competition (such as covering an opponent one-on-one and running the bases). Second, an athlete will be able to recover from the long-term effects of repetitive, energy-depleting skill demands throughout an entire competition (such as continually moving up and down the court and doing a series of high-intensity efforts). Finally, an athlete will adapt to the movement demands of the competition. General running, sprinting, reaction/quickness drills, agility drills and other sport-related drill work will expose an athlete to all activity demands.

Regarding speed improvement, to become faster at sprinting, an athlete should practice sprinting as fast as possible. Because most athletic competitions require "multi-directional" speed, however, spending a great deal of time on straight-line sprinting and traditional "speed-improvement" drills can be a waste of time for many athletes. This is why investing more time on agility and sport-related drills that replicate the demands of competition is recommended.

## TYPES OF METHODS

The sports-conditioning program should utilize a number of sport-related efforts/drills for adaptation to sport demands and development of specific energy systems. A comprehensive program not only develops total conditioning, it can also add variety to make it more tolerable.

The various options that make up a comprehensive program include interval training, sprint training and functional speed and agility drills.

### Interval Training

In essence, interval training is a series of efforts done for various lengths, target times and recovery periods. This type of training develops cardiorespiratory endurance by elevating the heart rate/work level during each effort and then allowing it to drop during the recovery period. The bouts are repeated for the designated number of times that are scheduled.

Brief guidelines and examples of interval training for running are as follows:

- Long Intervals – run distances of about 301 - 900 yards/meters. For instance, an athlete would do eight 340-yard runs (8 x 340 yd) or four 600-meter runs (4 x 600 m).

- Short Intervals – run distances of about 61 - 300 yards/meters. For instance, an athlete would run 14 110-yard sprints (14 x 110 yd) or eight 200-meter sprints (8 x 200 m).

- Shuttle Runs – run to one point then return to the start and repeat the procedure until the total distance is accomplished. For instance, a 200-yard shuttle done on a football field would involve running from the goal line to the 25-yard line and back to the goal line a total of four consecutive times.

- Aerobic Intervals – do long and short intervals at a lower-intensity pace with a limited recovery period between each effort. For instance, an athlete would perform eight 440-yard runs (8 x 400 yd) with a recovery period of about half the time that it takes to complete each run.

- Fartlek Training – do continuous laps around a track, court, football field or soccer field with varied striding, jogging and walking segments.

## Sprint Training

This type of training involves short-distance, maximum-effort sprints and/or technique drills that target straight-line sprinting ability. Normally, these should be performed with a full recovery between each effort to emphasize maximum intensity.

Brief guidelines and examples of sprint training for running are as follows:

- short sprints – run distances of about 20 - 60 yards (18.35 - 55 meters). For instance, an athlete would do 20 20-yard sprints (20 x 20 yd) or 15 36.5-meter sprints (15 x 36.5 m).
- sprint technique drills – do simplified sprint technique drills that address key mechanical components and improve correctable technique flaws.

## Functional Speed and Agility (FSA) Drills

Basically, FSA Drills are multi-directional/multi-pattern movement drills that address the various movement/change-of-direction/reaction situations that are encountered during a competition. They include forward running, backpedaling, lateral shuffling, planting, turning and reaction movements – all done as fast as possible while maintaining control and balance. A few examples of FSA Drills for running are as follows:

- Cone, Line and other Change-of-Direction (COD) Drills
- Reaction and Quickness (RAQ) Drills on a coach's command
- Position-Specific Drills (PSD) – sport-related run patterns/movements that are based upon playing position/sport demands
- Metabolic Agility Stations – COD, RAQ and PSD agility-type drills that are done in a station-to-station format that are intended to address cardiorespiratory endurance

Make note of this important point: Interval training, metabolic agility stations, sprint training and FSA Drills can enhance cardiorespiratory endurance as long as the heart rate is elevated, the recovery periods between bouts are minimized and an adequate number of bouts are performed. A "conditioning" effect can be obtained with these methods, making some training sessions more time-efficient. So, sprint training and FSA Drills can be combined for an endurance emphasis. This can facilitate more efficient training due to the limited amount of time that's available and the number of training components that need to be addressed.

## Miscellaneous Methods

Adding variety to the conditioning program can also facilitate improvement in fitness levels while minimizing boredom and drudgery. Periodic changes in efforts/drills, exercise prescriptions and training formats can sustain long-term positive results. Other ways and means by which variety can be added to training include the following:

- Vary the training week formats from one conditioning period to the next (such as switching the conditioning schedule from Monday/Wednesday/Friday to Tuesday/Thursday/Saturday).
- Choose either long, short, shuttle, aerobic or fartlek intervals.
- Use a variety of COD, RAQ and PSD Drills for FSA Training.
- Use short sprints, long sprints and/or technique drills for sprint training.
- Vary agility station drills along with station work:rest times.

## PRE-CONDITIONING WARM-UP/FLEXIBILITY ROUTINE

The purpose of the pre-conditioning warm-up/flexibility routine is to increase an athlete's core temperature and optimize her joint flexibility. Her body will then be able to function maximally and be less likely to become injured from the stresses encountered in the forthcoming workout. Going into a high-demand training session "cold" and inflexible will not permit maximum performance and may increase the risk of injury. Taking the time to properly warm up and stretch will facilitate the completion of a productive workout while minimizing the risk of injury.

The warm up/flexibility routine should consist of these elements:

- a five-minute jog or three- to four-lap jog around a football/soccer field, indoor/outdoor court or indoor/outdoor track
- a series of static-stretching exercises that address all major muscles/joints
- a variety of low-intensity, multi-dimensional, dynamic-movement drills

*Note:* On the days when high-level interval, sprint and/or FSA Training are scheduled, athletes should perform another segment of static-stretching exercises followed by a few more drills of higher-intensity movements.

## Long Dynamic-Movement Drill Routine

A long routine can be performed on higher-intensity days when short interval, shuttle, sprint or FSA Training is scheduled. This would be an example of a long dynamic-movement drill routine along with suggested distances and directions for an athlete:

- high knees (25 yards out, 25 yards back) – move forward, emphasizing high knees and arm-pumping action.
- butt kicks (15 yards out, 15 yards back) – move slowly, bringing the knee up to parallel to the ground in the front while touching the heel to the buttocks in the back on each step.

- drive-knee skips (25 yards out, 25 yards back) – skip forward, driving each lead knee upward while extending the rear leg forcefully off the ground (as in a long-jump take-off).
- backward reach (15 yards out, 15 yards back) – start facing away from the intended direction of movement, bending at the hips and knees. Raise the foot/heel to the buttocks then extend (stride) backward, covering as much distance as possible each step reaching backward.
- lateral shuffle (25 yards out, 25 yards back) – shuffle sideways, emphasizing low hips and a long sidestep. Don't move too quickly but be deliberate on each side step.
- high hurdle walk (15 yards out, 15 yards back) – walk forward as if stepping over high hurdles. Bring the lead knee out to the side, then up, around and down upon foot-ground contact.
- carioca with a high step (25 yards out, 25 yards back) – carioca sideways, emphasizing a big hip turn. When the rear leg moves to the front, emphasize a high knee sweep across the body.
- sprint accelerations (25 yards out, 25 yards back) – do 4 x 25-yard sprint accelerations coming out of a 40-yard dash stance or playing-position stance.

## Short Dynamic-Movement Drill Routine

The short routine can be performed on lower-intensity days when long intervals or aerobic work is scheduled. This would be an example of a short dynamic-movement drill routine (with each movement drill done over the same distance and as previously described):

- high knees
- lateral shuffle
- carioca with a high step
- backward reach
- butt kicks

## Pre-Conditioning Flexibility

A total-body flexibility routine should follow the jogging and dynamic-movement drills. The routine should take 5 - 10 minutes, depending upon the scheduled conditioning. A long flexibility routine should be performed on higher-intensity days when short interval, shuttle, sprint or FSA Training is scheduled; a shorter flexibility routine can be performed on lower-intensity days when long intervals or aerobic work is scheduled.

It's well beyond the scope of this chapter to provide detailed information about a flexibility program. However, several tips will be given that should be implemented by athletes for static stretching. (For a comprehensive look at stretching, you're encouraged to read the chapter "Improving Flexibility" by Rachael Picone in *The Female Athlete: Train for Success*.)

- Address the entire body, beginning with the torso and working downward. This makes the routine easier to learn and follow.
- Perform a two-phase progressive stretch for each exercise:
  - In the first phase, ease into the stretch and hold it for at least 10 seconds in a comfortable position. After the 10-second hold, totally relax and prepare for the second phase of the progressive stretch.
  - In the second phase, attempt to stretch a little farther than the position obtained in the initial stretch and hold it for another 10 seconds. Be cautious about overstretching the muscles.
- Concentrate on the muscles being stretched and feel them gradually lengthen.
- Stay relaxed throughout the routine. Having tension in the muscles will prevent you from obtaining a maximum stretch.
- Refrain from bouncing into the stretched position.

For the best results, the two most significant factors in a flexibility routine are (1) holding the stretch long enough to obtain a benefit and (2) consistent performance of the routine.

## POST-CONDITIONING COOL-DOWN

Following any conditioning session, a cool-down is highly recommended. For one thing, a cool-down assists in removing accumulated waste products from the muscles. This can facilitate the recovery process even when a minimum amount of time is invested. A few minutes of jogging and static-stretching exercises will suffice as an adequate cool-down.

## ADDITIONAL INGREDIENTS

Other relevant information regarding the implementation of a sound sports-conditioning program includes testing fitness levels and athletic ability, conditioning while injured, the conditioning benefit of circuit strength training and the importance of in-season conditioning.

### Testing

Various conditioning tests and athletic-ability assessments are traditionally utilized to measure the fitness levels and athleticism of athletes. Tests of cardiorespiratory endurance, speed, power, agility, flexibility and body composition along with some for athletic ability are relevant. However, not all tests assess sport-specific abilities accurately or the skill level that's required to perform well in actual competition.

If a conditioning test is used, it should reflect the demands of the predominant energy system(s) of a sport. In other words, it should be sport-related relative to the involvement of the ATP-PC, LA and/or Aerobic System(s). As an example, it would be rather foolish to assess sport-specific conditioning by having a softball player do a three-mile run or a gymnast do a 12-minute run because such tests are far-removed from the energy-system demand of each sport.

Relative to athletic ability and skill, a battery of tests are traditionally done to assess speed, power and agility. These include the 20/40-yard dash, vertical jump, standing long jump and a timed agility drill. These can be useful for assessing improvement that's made in an out-of-season training period if a pre-training test result is available for comparison. Since the tests aren't totally specific to skills and situations in competition, they may not truly reveal whom the best athletes are when it comes time to compete. But at least performing these tests does address some of the qualities that are needed for optimal athletic performance.

## Testing problems

Other than the aforementioned realities of testing, an athlete's genetic disposition plays a huge role in her ability. Naturally, those blessed with good genetics/natural ability can "put up better numbers" than those lacking the same degree of genetic prowess. One of the most frustrating situations for a coach is to have an athlete train hard but fail to show marked improvement on a designated day of testing because she isn't naturally gifted. To compound the issue is a genetically gifted athlete who failed to train hard but still managed to consistently "put up big numbers" that impress the head coach since this isn't a true reflection of her relative progress.

Even when an athlete may have worked out properly during a training period and should show improvement on the day of testing, she may test poorly due to a number of factors. She may be overtrained, not feeling well, be improperly warmed up or simply fail on the test trials (such as having a poor start in the 40-yard dash or using poor technique/form in the vertical or standing long jump).

Flexibility assessments – such as the sit-and-reach test for low-back/hamstring flexibility – can measure improvement, provided that a pre-test was done and the athlete addressed her low-back/hamstring flexibility on a consistent basis. However, due to anomalies in muscle/joint structures that may prohibit good flexibility in the lower back/hamstrings, some athletes will never show outstanding results in the sit-and-reach test. They simply aren't designed in a way that allows for even average flexibility in that area. Caution should be exercised when attempting to improve low-back/hamstring flexibility in those athletes who have these structural anomalies. They should avoid pushing/forcing their bodies beyond safe ranges of joint motion in an attempt to improve their flexibility.

Regarding body composition, testing body-fat percentages can create unnecessary psychological strain on certain athletes. Truly, some athletes are so concerned about their body-fat levels that they employ unsafe and/or ineffective nutritional and weight-loss tactics to attain some established "norm" for their sport or playing position. Understand that one's percentage of body fat is dependent upon a number of factors and optimal functional athletic ability can be attained regardless of whether or not a specific body-fat percentage or range of percentages is met.

## Sensible testing

The best "tests" for any athlete are her (1) record of attendance on all scheduled conditioning sessions and (2) level of effort in order to progress in all of the scheduled sessions regardless of the numbers that she produces on test day.

If testing is to be employed, it should reflect the demands/qualities required for a specific sport. Sensible testing should assess the predominant energy system of a sport and be as sport-related as possible. A pre-test is important to have something with which to compare and, furthermore, it should be relative to each athlete's improvement rather than a comparison between athletes. Making comparisons between athletes doesn't reflect accurately an athlete's relative improvement and work ethic. Instead, it favors those who are genetically gifted.

## Cardiorespiratory testing

Numerous options are available to accurately assess a large number of athletes "in the field" – that is, "outside the lab" – without having to use high-tech equipment for testing $VO_2$ max (maximum oxygen consumption). To be effective, the cardiorespiratory test should challenge athletes to meet a required target time that's based upon an individual's inherent running ability.

Tests of the Aerobic System include the following:

- 12-minute run – compare the distances covered in 12 minutes
- two-mile run – compare the times to complete the run
    Tests of the anaerobic systems include the following:
- 10 x 40-yard sprints with a recovery of 0:20 (20 seconds) between each sprint. (One option is to divide the fastest time in a 40-yard dash by the average time of all ten 40s to get a percentage. The higher the percentage, the better conditioned the athlete. Another option is to have all 40s within 5% of an athlete's fastest time in a 40-yard dash.)
- 16 x 110-yard sprints with a recovery of 0:45 between each sprint. (Athletes could be split into several groups based upon target times. For instance, target times could be 0:17 for a group of the fastest athletes, 0:19 for a group of the second-fastest athletes, 0:21 for a group of the third-fastest athletes and so on.)
- 2 x 300-yard shuttles with a recovery of two minutes between efforts. (Athletes could be split into several groups based upon target times. For instance, target times could be 0:58 for a group of the fastest athletes, 1:02 for a group of the second-fastest athletes, 1:06 for a group of the third-fastest athletes and so on.)
- 670-yard test on a football field using 50-, 120- and 500-yard segments with the cumulative time for each segment kept on a stopwatch). In Segment 1, an athlete would start at the goal line, sprint to the 25-yard line and back to the

goal line (for a total of 50 yards) then get a recovery period of 0:20. (Use a separate stopwatch to time the recovery.) In Segment 2, she would start from the goal line, sprint 60 yards to the far 40-yard line and back to the goal line (for a total of 120 yards) then get a recovery period of 0:40. In Segment 3, she would start at the goal line and run back and forth 100 yards from goal line to goal line five times (for a total of 500 yards) to complete the test. (Athletes could be split into several groups based upon target times to complete all three segments. For instance, target times could be 2:05 for a group of the fastest athletes, 2:13 for a group of the second-fastest athletes, 2:21 for a group of the third-fastest athletes and so on.)

## FSA Testing

Numerous tests can be used that employ a combination of straight-line speed and COD Drills. The run or drill should be easily measured and accurately timed. It's recommended that the times be measured electronically from start to finish with fully automated timing (FAT) to avoid the errors and variances that are common when timing by hand with a stopwatch.

Tests of speed include the following:

- 40-yard dash x 3 - 4 trials. This assures a reliable time in the event of a bad start, stumbling or poor effort. When timing by hand, use four stopwatches for each run. Discard the fastest and slowest times for each run and average the two times that remain. The 6 - 8 total times (two stopwatches x 3 - 4 trials each) can then be averaged.

- 10/20-yard sprints. These test pure starting speed along with speed in the initial stage of a run. FAT is highly recommended in these tests. If hand timing is used, follow the same procedures as noted for the 40-yard dash.

Tests of agility include the following:

- 5-10-5 Agility Drill. An athlete should run the drill (in a forward-run fashion) at least four times (four trials), twice going to the right and twice to the left. Record the average of the fastest time in each direction. Make sure the athlete starts in a three-point stance with her right hand down when going to the right and her left hand down when going to the left. It's also important that the athlete touches the end lines with her *hand*, not her foot. In other words, she should touch with her right hand when going right and her left hand when going left. It's highly recommended that FAT be used, preferably with a touch/sensor pad to start and end the drill.

- A multitude of agility drills can be used to assess agility. Any drill that confines an athlete into a relatively small area and requires her to perform quick and multiple changes of direction can be used provided that it can be run accurately and timed from start to finish. If backpedaling, lateral shuffling or other movements are incorporated, make sure that the athletes perform the movements in the correct manner without cheating.

### Strength/power/explosion testing

The functional display of muscular strength can be assessed using explosive but safe bodyweight-propelling tests. Tests of vertical and horizontal explosiveness include the following:

- Vertical jump. This assessment of vertical explosiveness can be done with the Vertec® testing device, a Just Jump® sensor pad or another device from a reputable manufacturer. An athlete should be given at least five trials to assure that she's warmed up and has adapted to the skill of vertical jumping. Taking a step prior to the actual jump – that is, stepping back then stepping forward just before the downward countermovement of the jump – can increase jump height. Normally, a no-step rule is employed to assure testing reliability and standardize the procedure. Whatever the case, be consistent in the procedures for the sake of accuracy and reliability.

- Standing long jump. This assessment of horizontal explosiveness is done best on a flat, semi-resilient surface such as an indoor/outdoor track or artificial turf (one that's unlike natural grass). A starting line must be marked and either a measuring tape or marked strip of tape is positioned perpendicular to the starting line. An athlete must begin behind the starting line, jump forward explosively, tuck her feet and attempt to land as far as possible from the starting line. The distance of the jump should be measured from the starting line to the heel of the foot that lands nearest to the starting line. Each athlete should be allowed 4 - 5 trials to assure that she has adapted to the skill and technique and to account for any improper jumps (such as falling backward upon landing, placing part of her foot over the starting line and so on).

### CONDITIONING WHEN INJURED

There are going to be times when an athlete sustains an injury that precludes her from participating in regularly scheduled conditioning workouts or team practices. In most cases, she can continue to condition but with restrictions applied.

Depending upon the type, magnitude and location of an injury, substitute methods of exercise can be used. The more severe the injury, the more care and caution should be taken to work around it. Also, depending upon the length of time that an athlete is expected to fully recover from an injury, a conditioning schedule can be developed to keep her active and minimize regression of her existing level of fitness.

If an athlete cannot run, she may be able to bike, walk or use a treadmill or another cardiorespiratory machine. If an athlete has a leg in a supportive device/cast, she may be able to bike with one leg and/or be restricted to upper-body exercises. Figure 9.12 offers some guidelines and conditioning considerations relative to an injured body part. (A detailed discussion of how to train an injured body part is given in Chapter 8.)

| BODY PART INJURED | OPTIONS FOR MINOR INJURIES | OPTIONS FOR MAJOR INJURIES |
|---|---|---|
| Neck | · jogging (easy)<br>· bicycle ergometer<br>· treadmill ergometer | · bicycle ergometer (restricted)<br>· walking |
| Shoulder | · jogging (easy)<br>· bicycle ergometer<br>· treadmill ergometer | · bicycle ergometer (with one arm or no arms)<br>· walking |
| Elbow | · running<br>· bicycle ergometer<br>· treadmill ergometer | · bicycle ergometer (with one arm or no arms)<br>· treadmill ergometer |
| Wrist | · running<br>· bicycle ergometer<br>· treadmill ergometer | · jogging (easy)<br>· bicycle ergometer (with one arm or no arms)<br>· treadmill ergometer |
| Lower Back/Hip | · bicycle ergometer (restricted) | · limited activity<br>· upper-body ergometer |
| Knee | · bicycle ergometer (with one leg) | · limited activity<br>· upper-body ergometer |
| Ankle | · bicycle ergometer (with one leg) | · bicycle ergometer (with one leg)<br>· upper-body ergometer |

**FIGURE 9.12: GUIDELINES AND CONDITIONING CONSIDERATIONS RELATIVE TO AN INJURED BODY PART**

The same concepts apply when an athlete is injured during an in-season period. A structured reconditioning program should be administered for athletes who aren't competing because of injuries that are sustained during the competitive season. This will facilitate an easier transition for them when they return to competition.

## Protocol for patello-femoral injury

Although hip, ankle and upper-body injuries can create limitations in conditioning methods, a major concern – and very common situation – pertains to patello-femoral restrictions. Naturally, the type of conditioning methods that are employed could have an adverse effect on the structural integrity of the knee joint. Here are some suggestions for reducing the risk of patello-femoral injures:

• Refrain from performing high-impact, high-force, jump-type activities/exercises due to the levels of stress that they place upon the joints. Over time, even less stressful methods – such as agility drills and straight-line running – can lead to excessive stress on the knees and increase the potential for injury.

• Avoid excessive running of stadium steps.

- Pedal the bicycle ergometer with the seat in a high position to increase the angle at the knee. The pedaling resistance should be minimal. In general, any agility-type drill – COD or RAQ – or any type of running that's performed by those with a history of knee problems should be done with caution.

## CIRCUIT STRENGTH TRAINING

Circuit strength training – where the strength-training workout is completed with minimal recovery between exercises and sets – elevates and sustains the heart rate to impose a high metabolic demand on the body. This type of training can be considered to be a "total-package" workout: Not only is muscular strength addressed but cardiorespiratory endurance is targeted as well – and without the excessive pounding on the joints that's associated with running activities. Essentially, a conditioning day can be obtained in the weight room because the demanding circuit is analogous to demanding interval training. A running day that's accounted for in the weight room allows more time for other concerns and can reduce the volume of training if a break from the normal routine is needed.

Any strength-training workout can be considered to be a circuit. What makes it a true circuit, however, is the less-than-normal recovery period between exercises and sets. There are a number of ways to minimize the recovery time, either by actual clock time or the sequence of exercises that are used. Here are some examples:

- Allow no more than about 30 - 45 seconds of recovery between all sets and exercises.
- Superset the exercises – that is, alternate the pushing and pulling movements – with about 15 - 20 seconds of recovery between them.
- Superset upper-body and lower-body movements with about 15 - 20 seconds of recovery between them.
- Use a push/pull-leg format – where an athlete moves from an upper-body pushing movement to an upper-body pulling movement to a lower-body movement with about 15 - 20 seconds of recovery between them.

## IN-SEASON CONDITIONING

Undoubtedly, it's critical to stay in good condition during the competitive season – especially near the end when playoffs/post-season competitions are important. Many injuries can occur not only in the latter part of a contest but at the end of the competitive season when the cumulative effects of fatigue can be a factor. When fatigue begins to set in, the inability to maximally contract muscles to stabilize joints occurs. Being sluggish and tired may mean that an athlete cannot move with alacrity to avoid potentially dangerous situations in competition such as collisions with other players, falling to the ground or any awkward twisting/turning movements.

## Weekend Competition (two options)

| SUNDAY | MONDAY | TUESDAY | WEDNESDAY | THURSDAY | FRIDAY | SATURDAY |
|---|---|---|---|---|---|---|
| | | Conditioning | Conditioning | | | Competition |

| SUNDAY | MONDAY | TUESDAY | WEDNESDAY | THURSDAY | FRIDAY | SATURDAY |
|---|---|---|---|---|---|---|
| | Conditioning | | Conditioning | | | Competition |

## Multiple Competitions per Week

| SUNDAY | MONDAY | TUESDAY | WEDNESDAY | THURSDAY | FRIDAY | SATURDAY |
|---|---|---|---|---|---|---|
| | | Competition | Conditioning | | Competition | Conditioning |

| SUNDAY | MONDAY | TUESDAY | WEDNESDAY | THURSDAY | FRIDAY | SATURDAY |
|---|---|---|---|---|---|---|
| Conditioning | | | Competition | Conditioning | | Competition |

## Mid-week Competition

| SUNDAY | MONDAY | TUESDAY | WEDNESDAY | THURSDAY | FRIDAY | SATURDAY |
|---|---|---|---|---|---|---|
| | Conditioning | | Competition | | Conditioning | |

**FIGURE 9.13: SUGGESTIONS FOR POST-PRACTICE SCHEDULING BASED UPON COMPETITIONS**

To an extent, maintaining optimal levels of conditioning throughout the season can be facilitated through practices and competitions. Clearly, a certain degree of conditioning can be obtained from the repetitive nature of practice sessions and the intensity of competition. However, some type of post-practice conditioning should be performed periodically to guarantee that athletes remain in good condition.

To be well recovered and prepared for a contest, any conditioning should occur well in advance of the actual competition. Some suggestions for post-practice scheduling based upon competition(s) are shown in Figure 9.13.

## Options

The conditioning options for an in-season period depend upon (1) the intensity level of the scheduled practice sessions and (2) the day of the next competition. On low-intensity/easier practice days, post-practice conditioning can be scheduled since it can be done when the athletes aren't overly fatigued. Regarding upcoming competitions, try to maintain a two-day/48-hour gap between post-practice conditioning and the competition to avoid overtaxing the recovery abilities of the athletes.

A variety of options can be used provided that they're done with proper intensity for the established distance/time. They can be conducted on the field, court or diamond in a minimal amount of time. Here are some options from which to choose going from lower repetitions/longer runs to higher repetitions/shorter runs:

- 2 - 3 repetitions of 120- to 150-yard intervals or shuttle runs
- 10 - 15 minutes of fartlek training
- 4 - 5 repetitions of 90- to 120-yard intervals or shuttle runs
- 5 - 10 minutes of fartlek training
- 6 - 7 repetitions of 70- to 100-yard intervals or shuttle runs
- 8 - 10 repetitions of 50- to 80-yard intervals or shuttle runs

## CONCLUDING REMARKS

The essence of sports conditioning is to enable athletes to perform at their maximum potential in each athletic competition over the course of an entire season. Proper planning and implementation of safe and practical conditioning methods and protocols will elevate each athlete's ability to accomplish this goal. A thorough understanding of the science behind conditioning and its program fundamentals will help coaches and athletes design and conduct an effective sport-related program. This chapter offers a simplistic overview of the science of sports conditioning and practical examples of how to implement sensible methods.

## REFERENCES

Bouchard, C., R. J. Shepard, T. Stephens, J. R. Sutton and B. D. McPherson. 1990. *Exercise, fitness, and health*. Champaign, IL: Human Kinetics.

Dudley, G., and T. Murray. 1982. *Energy for sport*. NSCA Journal 4 (3):14-15.

Edington, D. W., and V. R. Edgerton. 1976. *Biology of activity*. Boston, MA: Houghton-Mifflin.

Fleck, S., and W. Kraemer. 1987. *Designing resistance training programs*. Champaign, IL: Human Kinetics.

Jones, N. L., N. McCartney and A. J. McComas. eds. 1986. *Human muscle power*. Champaign, IL: Human Kinetics.

McFarlane, B. 1983. *Use of proper energy systems in training*. Track Technique 84.

Murray, B. 1980. *Interval training and specificity*. Track Technique 90.

Wilmore, J., and D. Costill. 1988. *Training for sport and activity*. Dubuque, IA: W. C. Brown.

# 10

# Progressive Interval Conditioning

*Tom Kelso, M.S., S.C.C.C., C.S.C.S.*

A program of progressive interval conditioning is based upon four increasingly challenging "levels" of exercise prescriptions for a variety of interval work (which usually involves running). The goal of the program is for athletes to progress over the course of an out-of-season training period from the easier Level 1 Workouts to the more demanding Level 2 and 3 Workouts and possibly attempting Level 4 Workouts (if appropriate). By doing this, it will be a good indication that they've adapted to the demands of each level, improved their fitness and, consequently, are in good condition which, then, makes them better able to face the demands of their competitive season.

In general, Level 1 Workouts are characterized by less bouts of exercise, lower relative running speeds and a greater amount of recovery between bouts. Level 1 Workouts are normally used in the early stages of out-of-season training and/or when athletes have done little or no conditioning for a significant period of time. Level 2 and 3 Workouts are characterized by more bouts of exercise, higher relative running speeds and a lower amount of recovery between bouts. Level 4 Workouts are the most challenging due to their greater volume (bouts of exercise) and running speed combined with shorter amounts of recovery between bouts. Only athletes who are in exceptional condition should attempt these workouts – those who have progressed to and mastered Level 3 Workouts. (*Note*: Even though the preceding and ensuing discussions of interval conditioning use running as examples, the concepts can be applied to virtually any mode of conditioning as well as any type of equipment.)

## INTERVAL OPTIONS

In this program, the interval options are categorized by venue and type of interval/shuttle and include a wide range of distances. Examples of interval options are given in Figure 10.1.

## TARGET TIMES AND GROUPING ATHLETES: THE RATIONALE

To create an overload while interval training (aside from manipulating the recovery time and number of bouts), a certain level of speed/effort should be exhibited that not only corresponds to the distance, time and nature of the run being performed but also to the individual performing the run. With each person being different, individualizing an athlete's level of speed/effort relative to her ability should, therefore, be done to obtain maximum benefits.

| VENUE | TYPE OF INTERVAL/SHUTTLE: DISTANCES |
|---|---|
| outdoor 400-meter track | long intervals: 800 and 400 meters |
| | short intervals: 200 and 100 meters |
| soccer/football field(53 x 120 yards) | long intervals: 680 and 345 yards |
| | short intervals: 200 and 100 yards |
| soccer field (college-size, fence at 200 feet) | long intervals: 530 and 265 yards |
| | short intervals: 140 and 120 yards |
| basketball court (college-size) | long shuttles: 125, 94 and 63 yards |
| | side shuttle: 33 yards |
| volleyball court | long shuttles: 80 and 60 yards |
| | side shuttles: 40 and 20 yards |
| tennis court | long shuttles: 101, 52 and 38 yards |
| | side shuttle: 24 yards |

**FIGURE 10.1: INTERVAL OPTIONS**

The most practical means by which to do this is based upon an athlete's natural ability to run. An athlete's ability to run a given distance is related largely to her maximum sprinting speed that's determined typically by the time that it takes to run the 40-yard dash. For example, consider these two athletes: Athlete 1 has the ability to sprint 40 yards in 4.90 seconds while Athlete 2 has the ability to sprint that distance in 5.70 seconds. If these two athletes were to race at distances of up to about 800 meters, Athlete 1 would most likely have an advantage over Athlete 2 (all other factors being equal).

Although not a perfect science, setting target times based upon an athlete's speed in the 40-yard dash can be more accurate than traditional methods of grouping athletes by body type or playing position. Assigning a 170-pound female who's relatively fast to a "slow" running group that consists of other athletes who are of the same/similar body type and/or playing position would mean that she'd have little difficulty achieving the target times for that group. Stated otherwise, she'd be running below her potential and not creating an optimal overload. Likewise, assigning a smaller female who's relatively slow to a "fast" running group that consists of other athletes who are of the same/similar body type and/or playing position would mean that she'd have much difficulty achieving the target times for that group. Because of disparities in body types and playing positions, using the speed in the 40-yard dash as a measuring device can be a more accurate tool when assigning athletes to running groups/target times.

In this program, the target times that are used for all interval levels are based upon an average time within a range. These averages are used to calculate target times based upon the distance of a run and a relative running speed that should be used during the run for a maximum training effect. The averages are shown in Table 10.1. When administering the interval workouts, knowing the speed of athletes – or timing them in a series of 40-yard dashes to determine their ability – will allow for them to be grouped in accordance with their needs.

| GROUP | RANGE OF TIMES | TARGET TIMES |
|:---:|:---:|:---:|
| 1 | 4.70 - 5.09 | 4.90 |
| 2 | 5.10 - 5.49 | 5.30 |
| 3 | 5.50 - 5.89 | 5.70 |
| 4 | 5.90 - 6.29+ | 6.10 |

**TABLE 10.1: AVERAGE RANGE OF TIMES FOR THE 40-YARD DASH**
Notes: (1) these times are for women and (2) the target times are based upon a percentage of the average times.

## Adjusting Target Times

It may be necessary to switch athletes who fall at either end of the time range for their running group to either a slower or faster group. As an example, an athlete in Group 1 who has the ability to run the 40-yard dash in 5.05 seconds (the "slow" end of the time range for Group 1) may find it difficult to make the target times based upon the standard 4.90 average that's used. In this case, she can be moved to Group 2. Similarly, an athlete in Group 3 who has the ability to run the 40-yard dash in 5.55 seconds (the "fast" end of the time range for Group 3) may find it easy to make the target times based upon the standard 5.70 average that's used. In this case, she can be moved to Group 2. The only way to determine whether or not athletes need to switch groups is by observing them during their conditioning workouts. Those athletes who consistently fail to achieve their target times or are unchallenged by them can be moved accordingly.

## RUNNING AT AN OPTIMAL PACE

The ultimate goal for an athlete is to run at her highest level of speed for any given distance. The following statement should make sense: The shorter the distance, the faster the relative running speed and the longer the distance, the slower the relative running speed (since it's literally impossible to maintain 100% speed when running longer distances). Whatever the case, the goal still should be to run as fast as possible for the prescribed distance.

Generally speaking, the goal of a sensible conditioning program is to progressively train an athlete so that she can sustain maximum speed for the greatest amount of time over any given distance. Therefore, with 40-yard dash speed being used as 100%, each interval option is based upon a percentage of this maximum speed relative to that particular distance and level. Low-level workouts are done with a lower percentage of maximum speed and high-level workouts are done with a higher percentage of maximum speed (to make them more challenging).

In the first few weeks of a conditioning program, an athlete with the ability to run a 40-yard dash in 5.20 seconds may find it challenging to complete a Level 1 Workout that consists of running 4 x 340-yard intervals (on a soccer/ football field) at a target time of 1:08 (per 340-yard interval) – the equivalent of running at 50% of her maximum speed. As the athlete progressively increases her level of fitness over the training period, she should be able to complete the 340-yard intervals at a higher level in the latter weeks. For instance, if she completes a Level 3 Workout that consists of running 7 x 340-yard intervals at a target time of 0:59 (per 340-yard interval) – the equivalent of running at 70% of her maximum speed – she obviously has improved her level of fitness.

## INTERVAL OPTION DETAILS

Athletes must train progressively and their workouts must be conducted properly (based upon the number of athletes who are running and their different abilities). In order to do so, it's important to understand the specific details of each interval option. These include the . . .

- type of interval (such as short, long, shuttle and so on)
- distance and description of the interval (such as the length as well as where and how to run it)
- level of each workout (such as 1, 2, 3 or 4)
- number of repetitions to run along with the total distance that's covered over the course of the workout
- percentage of maximum speed upon which the target times are based
- work:rest ratio (which is already calculated into the recovery times)
- target times for each group (GP) of athletes with different running abilities
- recovery times for each group (if running single groups of similar abilities or multiple groups of different abilities)
- run pace per lap/segment to aid in monitoring the proper running speed for each target time (if applicable)

A sample prescription that includes these details is shown in Figure 10.2. This example is for 200-yard short intervals on a soccer/football field (100 yards down and back). Here's a detailed breakdown of each category that's shown in the table:

- LEVEL: The "2" indicates that it's a Level 2 Workout (which is moderately difficult).
- REPS: The "7" refers to the number of repetitions/runs. Note that the workout involves a total distance of 1,400 yards [7 reps x 200 yards/rep].
- % SPEED: The "72.5" refers to the percentage of maximum speed at which the intervals should be done.
- W:R RATIO: The "1:3.5" indicates the work:rest ratio to be used (which has already been factored into the recovery times). Specifically, this means that the recovery period between each work interval should be 3.5 times the duration of the work interval.
- TARGET TIME: This is the time for which to aim based upon running abil-

ity/percent speed for different abilities. Note that four groups are listed with their target times (GP1 = 0:33, GP2 = 0:35, GP3 = 0:37 and GP4 = 0:40).

- RECOVERY TIME (*left* side of column): These are the recovery times if single abilities are run separately. Note that recovery times are listed for four groups (GP1 = 1:54, GP2 = 2:02, GP3 = 2:12 and GP4 = 2:20).

- RECOVERY TIME (*right* side of column, in parenthesis/brackets): This is the recovery time if different abilities are run in the same session. But in different groups, the options are as follows:

  - If running one group of varied abilities – that is, fast and slow athletes together – use the recovery time of (1 = 2:07). This is the time that elapses before the entire group should run the next interval.

  - If running two different ability groups separately – such as GP1 and GP2 combined into Group A and GP3 and GP4 combined into Group B – use the recovery time of [2 = 1:31]. This is the time that elapses after Group B finishes their interval before Group A starts its next interval.

  - If running three different ability groups separately – such as GP1 in Group A, GP2 and GP3 combined into Group B and GP4 in Group C – use the recovery time of {3 = 0:54}. This is the time that elapses after Group C finishes their interval before Group A starts its next interval.

- RUN PACE @ 100 YARDS: This is the time for each group at the halfway point of the run (100 yards) to be on pace to achieve the target time.

| LEVEL | REPS (TOTAL DISTANCE) | % SPEED | W:R RATIO | TARGET TIME | RECOVERY | TIME | RUN PACE @ 100 YARDS |
|---|---|---|---|---|---|---|---|
| 2 | 7 (1,400 yards) | 72.5 | 1:3.5 | GP1 = 0:33 | 1:54 | (1 = 2:07) | 0:17 |
| | | | | GP2 = 0:35 | 2:02 | [2 = 1:31] | 0:18 |
| | | | | GP3 = 0:37 | 2:12 | {3 = 0:54} | 0:19 |
| | | | | GP4 = 0:40 | 2:20 | | 0:20 |

FIGURE 10.2: SAMPLE PRESCRIPTION

## PROGRESSION OPTIONS

The appendix details 24 interval workouts using a variety of venues and distances. Level 1 Workouts should be scheduled in the initial weeks of the training period when an athlete's level of fitness is lower than optimal. As the training period progresses and she improves her fitness, more challenging Level 2 and 3 Workouts should then be attempted. If an athlete is in exceptional condition and is able to tolerate Level 3 Workouts, she can progress to Level 4 Workouts.

The "long-to-short" method of progression can be practical. Longer-duration, lower-intensity workouts are performed in the initial weeks of the training period working toward shorter-duration, higher-intensity workouts in the latter weeks as the competitive season approaches.

There are two methods of progression: similar and varied. Two options for each method are as follows:

## Option 1: Similar-Method Progression

Long-to-short, similar-method progression entails using similar types of intervals and progressing from Level 1 Workouts on up. Examples of this are shown in Figures 10.3 (on a basketball court) and 10.4 (on a soccer/football field).

| WEEKS | INTERVALS | | LEVEL |
|-------|-----------|---|-------|
| 1 - 2 | 125-yard long shuttles | *venue: basketball court* | 1 |
| 3 - 5 | 94-yard long shuttles | *venue: basketball court* | 2 |
| 6 - 7 | 63-yard long shuttles | *venue: basketball court* | 3 |

**FIGURE 10.3: EXAMPLE ONE OF SIMILAR-METHOD PROGRESSION**

| WEEKS | INTERVALS | | LEVEL |
|-------|-----------|---|-------|
| 1 - 4 | 680-yard long interals | *venue: soccer/football field* | 1 & 2 |
| 5 - 9 | 340-yard long interals | *venue: soccer/football field* | 3 & 4 |

**FIGURE 10.4: EXAMPLE TWO OF SIMILAR-METHOD PROGRESSION**

## Option 2: Varied-Method Progression

Long-to-short, varied-method progression entails using varied types of intervals in some combination and progressing from Level 1 Workouts on up. Examples of this are shown in Figures 10.5 (on an outdoor track and a soccer/football field) and 10.6 (on a volleyball court).

| WEEKS | INTERVALS | | LEVEL |
|-------|-----------|---|-------|
| 1 - 3 | long intervals: 800 and 400 meters | *venue: 400-meter track* | 1 |
| 4 - 5 | short intervals: 200 and 100 meters | *venue: 400-meter track* | 1 & 2 |
| 6 - 7 | short intervals: 200 yards | *venue: soccer/football field* | 2 & 3 |
| 8 - 10 | short intervals: 100 yards | *venue: soccer/football field* | 3 & 4 |

**FIGURE 10.5: EXAMPLE ONE OF VARIED-METHOD PROGRESSION**

| WEEKS | INTERVALS | | LEVEL |
|-------|-----------|---|-------|
| 1 - 2 | 80-yard long shuttles | *venue: volleyball court* | 1 & 2 |
| 3 - 5 | 80- and 60-yard long shuttles | *venue: volleyball court* | 2 & 3 |
| 6 - 8 | 40- and 20-yard long shuttles | *venue: volleyball court* | 3 |

**FIGURE 10.6: EXAMPLE TWO OF VARIED-METHOD PROGRESSION**

## ADMINISTERING INTERVAL WORKOUTS TO GROUPS

Interval workouts can be administered to the four separate groups individually or to multiple groups simultaneously (all groups/abilities run together in the same workout session). Individually, a group of athletes with similar abilities would complete the entire workout as prescribed; simultaneously, athletes with differing abilities would run together (but in separate running groups) with their target and recovery times adjusted accordingly. Due to varied recovery times, however, it's impossible to precisely run all four groups simultaneously in succession for most of the prescribed workouts. In other words, if a coach runs the groups in a particular order – such as Group 1, 2, 3 and 4 – and then repeats the sequence, the recovery time for some groups would, invariably, either be shortened or lengthened and deviate from the exact exercise prescriptions that are listed.

For all practical purposes – and for the sake of time-management – every one of the prescribed workouts can be performed by combining all of the athletes into one, two or three different running groups based upon ability. Although recovery times will deviate from the norm, it's more practical to conduct workouts this way – especially when training a large number of athletes. With this in mind, there are several options available for administering workouts to single groups and multiple groups.

## Single Groups

Here are three options for using exact recovery times:

- Run each group separately. Do the entire workout for Group 1 by itself, then Groups 2, 3 and 4. This may not be practical if time is limited.
- Run all groups at the same time in separate areas and with the help of others timing each group. This is feasible if the groups run length-wise on the soccer/football field or court. But if the groups run perimeter-wise on the soccer/football field or track, it may create too much congestion.
- Establish a workout schedule so that each group trains at a different time during the day.

## Multiple Groups

Sometimes it isn't possible to run individual groups by themselves with the exact recovery times as in the three previous examples. Another option, then, is that all four groups can run simultaneously in succession and in varied groups – provided that the recovery times are averaged. (Note that averaging is already factored into the interval prescriptions that are listed.) To an extent, this will lengthen the normal recovery times for Groups 1 and 2 and shorten the normal recovery times for Groups 3 and 4. The recovery times will not be precise relative to exact work:rest ratios. However, workouts can be completed in a more practical and time-efficient manner by using this averaging method.

As an example, refer to the prescription in the appendix for doing 94-yard long shuttles on a basketball court. The Level 3 Workout involves 14 repetitions with these target times: Group 1 = 0:16.5, Group 2 = 0:18.0, Group 3 = 0:19.0 and Group 4 = 0:20.0. Here are three different options for using average recovery times:

- Use one combined-ability running group. Here, all athletes run at the same time – regardless of ability – with each athlete aiming for her specific target time. Note that the recovery time for this method – as shown on the right side of the column for recovery time – is designated as "(1 = 1:04)." The recovery time should begin when the last runner finishes or when the work time on the stopwatch reaches the average of all target times (approximately 0:18.0). When using this method, a second stopwatch will be necessary. In this case, the recovery interval should begin even though some athletes may still be running and others have finished. When the recovery time of 1:04 has elapsed on the second stopwatch, all athletes should start on the next interval.

- Use two different-ability running groups. The two groups can be Group A (with Group 1 and 2 abilities) and Group B (with Group 3 and 4 abilities). The target times remain the same as if running the four groups separately. Group A would run first followed immediately by Group B. After Group B completes the interval, begin the recovery time that's designated as "[2 = 0:46]." When this recovery time has elapsed, start Group A on its second interval. When they finish, immediately start Group B. When Group B finishes, repeat the recovery interval of 0:46 and continue this procedure until all runs are completed.

- Use three different-ability running groups. The three groups can be Group A (with Group 1 ability), Group B (with Group 2 and 3 abilities combined or simply Group 2 ability by itself) and Group C (with Group 4 ability or, if Group 2 ability alone is used for the second group, Group 3 and 4 abilities combined). Again, the target times remain the same as if running the four groups separately. Run Groups A, B and C in succession. After Group C completes the interval, begin the recovery time that's designated as "{3 = 0:27}." When this recovery time has elapsed, run the groups in succession again followed by the recovery interval of 0:27. Continue this procedure until all runs are completed.

## CONCLUDING REMARKS

One of the goals of a sound program of conditioning is to train progressively. As the athletes adapt to existing levels, the workout demands should increase. In this manner, athletes will be better prepared to take on the demands of athletic competition. By following the pre-designed progressive interval levels suggested in this chapter, the conditioning levels of athletes can be maximized to enhance their athletic performance.

# 11

# Scheduling and Organization: Implementing a Year-Round Program

*John Rinaldo, B.S.*

One of the most difficult tasks that a strength coach can face lies in the logistical nightmare of scheduling and organizing year-round strength training, conditioning and agility/speed programs for scholastic or collegiate athletes. The variables that make the task so potentially arduous is the number of teams; their constituent athletes; their specific time constraints due to class scheduling; the availability of the strength staff; the time restrictions due to faculty/staff use; the possibility that the facility isn't only used by the athletic department but the entire student population; and, of course, the amount of training space and equipment that's available in the strength and conditioning facility. After factoring in or out any of the aforementioned variables, a coach also has to schedule workouts for strength training, conditioning and agility/speed when warranted. Since some high schools and colleges don't require every team to utilize the program and facilities, the scheduling of these components will depend upon the use of the strength and conditioning staff by various sports.

The purpose of this chapter, then, is to give the aspiring, novice or veteran coach a three-step framework for scheduling, organizing and implementing a year-round program that includes a variety of strength-training protocols, conditioning workouts and agility/speed training while dealing with variables that could affect a program's structure.

**It's important to plan workouts around practice and skill training. (Photo by Pete Silletti)**

## STEP 1: ASSESSING AND PLANNING

The initial step involves four main areas. This includes assessing the hours of scheduling, assessing team logistics, planning the program and developing the training calendar.

### Assessing the Hours of Scheduling

When setting up a program, the first thing to do is determine the weight-room hours and to track those hours as well as miscellaneous hours in the facility. There are, of course, variations but most collegiate weight rooms are open from six in the morning to six in the evening, Monday through Friday, with optional hours on the weekend (all of which, naturally, depends upon the time of year). When determining the weight-room hours, make sure to take into account any coverage by the department staff – meaning the sport coaches and/ or their assistants – as well as the usage by the faculty/staff and general student population, if dictated by the department. If it is, the hours should be reserved for the facility highlighting these times; if it isn't, then the scheduling will be much easier. After the facility hours have been set, post them in a highly visible area and send a copy to each coach in the department so there will not be an issue with communication once workouts have been scheduled.

### Assessing Team Logistics

After establishing the facility hours, the next task is to assess individual team logistics. This is paramount if you're a coach who's scheduling any facility for team use. Some coaches prefer an "open" weight-room policy that allows athletes to come at their own whim. However, this makes it difficult for compliance and detracts from the philosophy of team training that's held by many coaches.

"Team logistics" refers to the details that may affect how a team can be scheduled during the school year. These details should cover as many variables as possible that could potentially interfere with any structured timetable. Questions to be asked include the following:

- How many teams will be using the facility?
- How long of a time period is needed for each team?
- What are the goals of each team? (In other words, how is the strength program important to them?)
- What are the practice schedules of the teams?
- What are the class schedules of the student-athletes?
- How much space is available to accommodate each team?
- Will teams need to be split up due to the size of the facility and equipment constraints?
- How many staff are available to cover each session?

As you're performing your assessment, make it a point to gather as much information as possible from each sport coach or the assistants. During this process, the key is having clear communication with each team. In addition, it may become apparent that some coaches aren't sufficiently organized to provide you with what you may need. So, be patient and keep a contact record for follow-up exchanges.

Once each team has been assessed in accordance with their needs, it's then important to list and prioritize the scheduling of each team based upon their size and where they're at in their training calendar (such as the off-season, in-season or pre-season). Teams that are larger will be more difficult to schedule because of their numbers, time constraints and internal scheduling. And in-season sports have practices and competitions that will affect their availability. In es-

A variety of strength-training protocols can be implemented for scholastic and collegiate athletics. (Photo by Pete Silletti)

sence, these teams should be given a higher priority for scheduling than teams that are smaller and/or in their off-seasons where they may have more leeway with their time.

## Planning the Program

Once the facility hours and team logistics have been assessed, the next thing to do is to plan the training calendar of each team for the year, then the semester (or quarter) and then the month. Even if a periodization model is used, the calendar should include off-season, in-season and pre-season programs. In order to accomplish this, a strength coach must know each team's in-season practice and playing schedules, pre-season practice schedules and off-season schedules for individual development. Additionally, a strength coach must know how much time is available for training sessions within the department. It's important to plan workouts around practice and skill training. Communication between the strength and conditioning staff and the coaching staff of each sport must be a priority. A strength coach should coordinate meetings with each team. Rather than waiting to be approached, a strength coach should take the initiative at the earliest opportunity.

Software applications for monthly planning, multi-faceted organizational programs and simple day planners are all great tools to assist and document any schedule. It's well beyond the scope of this discussion to provide examples of a 12-month calendar for every sport. However, an illustration of a year-round strength and conditioning program that's tailored for a women's collegiate basketball team is given at the end of this chapter. Once the concepts of scheduling and organization are understood, the calendar can be adapted to any sport at either the scholastic or collegiate level.

## Developing the Training Calendar

The final task in this step is to develop a training calendar. In doing so, there are several key points that must be addressed. Here are some considerations for pre-season, in-season and off-season training for a team that competes in the winter:

### Pre-season

- athletic training room schedules and rehab schedules
- athlete class and meeting schedules
- team meetings
- team meal schedules
- community service
- holidays
- semester breaks

### In-season

- team training and practice schedules
- competition schedules
- athletic training room schedules and rehab schedules
- athlete class and meeting schedules
- final exams
- team meal schedules
- travel schedules
- holidays
- semester breaks
- mandatory days off (as per national or state regulations)

### Off-season

- semester breaks
- work-study schedules
- athletic training room schedules and rehab schedules
- athlete class and meeting schedules
- individual skill-development sessions
- summer tournaments and facility availability

## STEP 2: ORGANIZING SCHEDULES

Once a strength coach has planned and developed schedules for each team, the current schedules can be posted in the facility and distributed to all of the coaches for every sport. Weekly meetings should be held with a representative from each sport staff to discuss potential changes. It's important to note that during the course of overlapping seasons, a variety of teams will have changes and conflicts. A strong, organized plan will assist in the management of a facility that has been prepared for such cases.

## STEP 3: IMPLEMENTING COMPONENTS

After the tasks of assessing and planning have been completed, the next step is to implement the program based upon needs. In any year-round program, there are several components to consider: strength training; sprint (or speed) training; agility training and plyometrics; anaerobic conditioning; and aerobic conditioning. (Anaerobic conditioning is a component of many – but not all – sports; some sports also incorporate yoga training.) The following information is an overview for scheduling each aspect of training along with some considerations.

### Strength Training

A variety of strength-training protocols can be implemented for scholastic and collegiate athletics. These are just a few variations of the many that are possible:

- total-body routine, one day/week
- total-body routine, two days/week
- total-body routine, three days/week (on non-consecutive days)
- split routine, three days/week (on non-consecutive days such as upper body on Monday, lower body on Wednesday and upper body on Friday then reversing it the next week)
- split routine, four days/week
- split routine, four days/weekend (such as upper body "push" on Wednesday and Saturday and upper body "pull" and lower body on Thursday and Sunday)

And while all of these programs have a common goal, it's up to a strength coach to delineate these accordingly during the off-season, pre-season and in-season programs. For example, the volume and frequency of training are traditionally greater in off-season programs and gradually decreased as the season draws near to allow for the added demands that are placed upon the athletes from practices. Note that changes in the frequency of training are illustrated in the year-round calendar that appears at the end of this chapter.

## Sprint (or Speed) Training

Typically, sprint (or speed) training is scheduled during the late off-season and pre-season programs. Since an athlete's level of anaerobic stress is elevated during sprint workouts, an adequate period of recovery should be programmed between each session. Coaches must remember that they aren't training an athlete for conditioning and the quality of recovery is integral to speed development. Also keep in mind that the fatigue levels and muscular damage that's produced by strength training will have an affect on both the quality of the sprint workout as well as recovery. It should be noted that any type of track or sod surface is preferred for these workouts; pure concrete surfaces should be avoided in order to reduce the potential for injury. Some coaches, however, may be handicapped by their track facility and may have to substitute speed workouts for a variety of aerobic modalities that are at their disposal. While these circumstances are more than acceptable, it's important to remember that a track or a treadmill is necessary to develop optimal running mechanics and improve sprint skills.

## Agility Training and Plyometrics

Scheduling agility drills (such as those involving quickness and change of direction) and plyometric drills (such as those involving jumping and bounding) are usually programmed for the same workout but should be scheduled on separate days from sprint training. The training for these skills needs to be performed in exclusive settings and during separate times (and perhaps separate days). Similar to sprint training, agility and plyometric training should be performed solely during the off-season and pre-season workouts because of the added demands of practice once the season is underway. But there are always exceptions and "micro-workouts" can be included at any time for athletes who strive to get better or for those whose skill development in these areas is below the norm.

## Anaerobic Conditioning

Depending upon the sport, anaerobic conditioning should be scheduled primarily toward the end of the off-season and pre-season training to help athletes develop a tolerance for fatigue and game-type situations. Athletes who compete in sports that involve repeated sprinting – such as soccer, lacrosse and basketball – would benefit enormously from having a variety of these workouts included in their training calendars. A multiplicity of drills can be designed to facilitate an anaerobic effect ranging from those that require agility and change of direction to plyometric drills to sprint training. The key is to manipulate the amount of recovery time between work intervals to achieve the desired effect.

## Aerobic Conditioning

For many years, aerobic conditioning has been used to achieve numerous purposes. In brief, aerobic conditioning forms the basis of recovery, off-sets fatigue for any form of anaerobic conditioning, facilitates in accelerating fat loss and serves as the function for increasing cardiac output. The majority of sports are anaerobic in nature. But it's imperative that athletes develop a strong base of aerobic support before engaging in anaerobic conditioning – preferably beginning in their off-season training. Knowing that athletes will be constrained by their training environments – such as the time of the year and the availability of training equipment – coaches should provide an assortment of modalities from which they can choose while undertaking this phase of the training program. Despite the fact that aerobic conditioning is primarily scheduled during the off-season program, special cases can always be determined during pre-season and in-season training for athletes who are overweight and/or poorly conditioned.

## CONCLUDING REMARKS

Planning, organizing and implementing a year-round strength and conditioning program may seem like an arduous task when taking into account all of the variables that are involved. However, it doesn't have to be provided that forethought, preparation and commitment are its foundation. At the end of the day, it's ultimately the initiative of any head strength coach and his/her staff in leading the way for the blueprint of success.

# August

# Women's Basketball: Off-Season Training

| SUNDAY | MONDAY | TUESDAY | WEDNESDAY | THURSDAY | FRIDAY | SATURDAY |
|---|---|---|---|---|---|---|
| | | | | | 1 | 2 |
| 3<br>Aerobic Conditioning (3-Mile Run) | 4<br>Strength Training Total Body | 5<br>Aerobic Conditioning Non-Running Activity (30:00) | 6<br>Speed Training and Anaerobic Conditioning | 7<br>Strength Training Total Body | 8<br>Aerobic Conditioning Non-Running Activity (30:00) | 9<br>Speed Training and Anaerobic Conditioning |
| 10<br>Aerobic Conditioning (3-Mile Run) | 11<br>Strength Training Total Body | 12<br>Aerobic Conditioning Non-Running Activity (30:00) | 13<br>Speed Training and Anaerobic Conditioning | 14<br>Strength Training Total Body | 15<br>Aerobic Conditioning Non-Running Activity (30:00) | 16<br>Speed Training and Anaerobic Conditioning |
| 17<br>Aerobic Conditioning (3-Mile Run) | 18<br>Strength Training Total Body | 19<br>Aerobic Conditioning Non-Running Activity (30:00) | 20<br>Speed Training and Anaerobic Conditioning | 21<br>Strength Training Total Body | 22<br>Aerobic Conditioning Non-Running Activity (30:00) | 23<br>Speed Training and Anaerobic Conditioning |
| 24<br>Aerobic Conditioning (3-Mile Run) | 25<br>Strength Training Total Body | 26<br>Aerobic Conditioning Non-Running Activity (30:00) | 27<br>Speed Training and Anaerobic Conditioning | 28<br>Strength Training Total Body | 29<br>Aerobic Conditioning Non-Running Activity (30:00) | 30<br>Speed Training and Anaerobic Conditioning |
| 31 | | | | | | |

# September
# Women's Basketball: Pre-Season Training

| SUNDAY | MONDAY | TUESDAY | WEDNESDAY | THURSDAY | FRIDAY | SATURDAY |
|---|---|---|---|---|---|---|
| | 1<br>Students Arrive on Campus | 2<br>7:00 AM: Strength Training Test | 3<br>Team Cardio | 4<br>Team Cardio | 5<br>7:00 AM: Strength Training | 6<br>Team Cardio Test (1-Mile Run) |
| 7 | 8<br>3:00 PM: Agililty Drills Strength Training | 9<br>7:00 AM: Sprint Training | 10<br>3:00 PM: Strength Training | 11<br>Team Cardio and Stretch Agility Drills | 12<br>3:00 PM: Strength Training | 13<br>10:00 AM: Sprint Training |
| 14 | 15<br>3:00 PM: Agililty Drills Strength Training | 16<br>7:00 AM: Sprint Training | 17<br>3:00 PM: Strength Training | 18<br>Team Cardio and Stretch Agility Drills | 19<br>3:00 PM: Strength Training | 20<br>10:00 AM: Sprint Training |
| 21 | 22<br>3:00 PM: Agililty Drills Strength Training | 23<br>7:00 AM: Sprint Training | 24<br>3:00 PM: Strength Training | 25<br>Team Cardio and Stretch Agility Drills | 26<br>3:00 PM: Strength Training | 27<br>10:00 AM: Sprint Training |
| 28 | 29<br>3:00 PM: Agililty Drills Strength Training | 30<br>7:00 AM: Sprint Training | | | | |
| | | | | | | |

# October
## Women's Basketball: Pre/In-Season Training

| SUNDAY | MONDAY | TUESDAY | WEDNESDAY | THURSDAY | FRIDAY | SATURDAY |
|---|---|---|---|---|---|---|
| | | | **1**<br>3:00 PM:<br>Strength<br>Training | **2**<br>Team Cardio<br>and Stretch<br>Agility Drills | **3**<br>3:00 PM:<br>Strength<br>Training | **4**<br>10:00 AM:<br>Sprint<br>Training |
| **5** | **6**<br>3:00 PM:<br>Agililty Drills<br>Strength Training | **7**<br>7:00 AM:<br>Sprint<br>Training | **8**<br>3:00 PM:<br>Strength<br>Training | **9**<br>Team Cardio<br>and Stretch<br>Agility Drills | **10**<br>3:00 PM:<br>Strength<br>Training | **11**<br>10:00 AM:<br>Sprint<br>Training |
| **12** | **13**<br>3:00 PM:<br>Agililty Drills<br>Strength Training | **14**<br>7:00 AM:<br>Sprint<br>Training | **15**<br>3:00 PM:<br>Strength<br>Training | **16**<br>Team Cardio<br>and Stretch<br>Agility Drill | **17**<br>3:00 PM:<br>Strength<br>Training | **18**<br>Practices<br>Begin |
| **19** | **20**<br>3:00 PM:<br>Agililty Drills<br>Strength Training | **21**<br>6:00 PM:<br>Agility<br>Training | **22** | **23**<br>6:00 PM:<br>Strength<br>Training | **24**<br>6:00 PM:<br>Agility<br>Training | **25** |
| **26** | **27**<br>3:00 PM:<br>Strength<br>Training | **28**<br>6:00 PM:<br>Agility<br>Training | **29** | **30**<br>6:00 PM:<br>Strength<br>Training | **31**<br>6:00 PM:<br>Agility<br>Training | |
| | | | | | | |

## November
## Women's Basketball: In-Season Training

| SUNDAY | MONDAY | TUESDAY | WEDNESDAY | THURSDAY | FRIDAY | SATURDAY |
|---|---|---|---|---|---|---|
| | | | | | | 1 |
| 2 6:00 PM: Strength Training | 3 | 4 GAME (HOME) | 5 | 6 6:00 PM: Strength Training | 7 | 8 GAME (HOME) |
| 9 | 10 6:00 PM: Strength Training | 11 | 12 | 13 6:00 PM: Strength Training | 14 | 15 GAME (HOME) |
| 16 | 17 6:00 PM: Strength Training | 18 | 19 | 20 6:00 PM: Strength Training | 21 | 22 GAME (AWAY) |
| 23 6:00 PM: Strength Training | 24 | 25 GAME (HOME) | 26 6:00 PM: Strength Training | 27 THANKSGIVING | 28 HOLIDAY TOURNAMENT (HOME) | 29 HOLIDAY TOURNAMENT (HOME) |
| 30 6:00 PM: Strength Training | | | | | | |

# December
# Women's Basketball: In-Season Training

| SUNDAY | MONDAY | TUESDAY | WEDNESDAY | THURSDAY | FRIDAY | SATURDAY |
|---|---|---|---|---|---|---|
| | 1 | 2<br>GAME<br>(AWAY) | 3<br>6:00 PM:<br>Strength<br>Training | 4 | 5<br>GAME<br>(HOME) | 6<br>6:00 PM:<br>Strength<br>Training |
| 7 | 8<br>GAME<br>(HOME) | 9<br>6:00 PM:<br>Strength<br>Training | 10 | 11<br>GAME<br>(AWAY) | 12<br>6:00 PM:<br>Strength<br>Training | 13 |
| 14 | 15<br>FINAL EXAMS<br>Strength<br>Training (opt.) | 16<br>FINAL EXAMS | 17<br>FINAL EXAMS | 18<br>FINAL EXAMS<br>Strength<br>Training (opt.) | 19<br>FINAL EXAMS | 20<br>12:00 PM:<br>Strength<br>Training |
| 21<br>WINTER<br>BREAK<br>BEGINS | 22<br>GAME<br>(HOME) | 23<br>3:00 PM:<br>Strength<br>Training | 24<br>CHRISTMAS<br>EVE | 25<br>CHRISTMAS | 26<br>3:00 PM:<br>Strength<br>Training | 27 |
| 28<br>TRAVEL DAY | 29<br>HOLIDAY<br>TOURNAMENT<br>(AWAY) | 30<br>HOLIDAY<br>TOURNAMENT<br>(AWAY) | 31<br>NEW YEAR'S<br>EVE<br>TRAVEL DAY | | | |
| | | | | | | |

# January
# Women's Basketball: In-Season Training

| SUNDAY | MONDAY | TUESDAY | WEDNESDAY | THURSDAY | FRIDAY | SATURDAY |
|---|---|---|---|---|---|---|
| | | | | **1** 6:00 PM: Strength Training | **2** | **3** GAME (HOME) |
| **4** 6:00 PM: Strength Training | **5** | **6** GAME (AWAY) | **7** DAY OFF | **8** 6:00 PM: Strength Training | **9** | **10** GAME (AWAY) |
| **11** | **12** 6:00 PM: Strength Training | **13** | **14** | **15** 6:00 PM: Strength Training | **16** | **17** GAME (HOME) |
| **18** WINTER BREAK ENDS | **19** 6:00 PM: Strength Training | **20** | **21** GAME (HOME) | **22** DAY OFF | **23** 6:00 PM: Strength Training | **24** |
| **25** | **26** 6:00 PM: Strength Training | **27** | **28** GAME (AWAY) | **29** 6:00 PM: Strength Training | **30** | **31** GAME (HOME) |
| | | | | | | |

# February
## Women's Basketball: In-Season Training

| SUNDAY | MONDAY | TUESDAY | WEDNESDAY | THURSDAY | FRIDAY | SATURDAY |
|---|---|---|---|---|---|---|
| 1 | 2<br>6:00 PM:<br>Strength<br>Training | 3 | 4<br>GAME<br>(AWAY) | 5<br>6:00 PM:<br>Strength<br>Training | 6 | 7<br>GAME<br>(HOME) |
| 8 | 9<br>6:00 PM:<br>Strength<br>Training | 10 | 11<br>GAME<br>(HOME) | 12<br>6:00 PM:<br>Strength<br>Training | 13 | 14<br>GAME<br>(AWAY) |
| 15 | 16<br>6:00 PM:<br>Strength<br>Training | 17 | 18<br>GAME<br>(AWAY) | 19<br>6:00 PM:<br>Strength<br>Training | 20 | 21<br>GAME<br>(HOME) |
| 22<br>6:00 PM:<br>Strength<br>Training | 23 | 24<br>GAME<br>(AWAY) | 25<br>6:00 PM:<br>Strength<br>Training | 26 | 27 | 28<br>GAME<br>(HOME) |
| 29 | | | | | | |
| | | | | | | |

## March
## Women's Basketball: In/Off-Season Training

| SUNDAY | MONDAY | TUESDAY | WEDNESDAY | THURSDAY | FRIDAY | SATURDAY |
|---|---|---|---|---|---|---|
| | 1<br>6:00 PM:<br>Strength<br>Training | 2 | 3 | 4<br>6:00 PM:<br>Strength<br>Training | 5 | 6<br>CONFERENCE<br>TOURNAMENT<br>(AWAY) |
| 7<br>CONFERENCE<br>TOURNAMENT<br>(AWAY) | 8<br>CONFERENCE<br>TOURNAMENT<br>(AWAY) | 9<br>CONFERENCE<br>TOURNAMENT<br>(AWAY) | 10 | 11 | 12 | 13 |
| 14 | 15<br>POST-SEASON<br>TOURNAMENT<br>(AWAY) | 16 | 17 | 18 | 19 | 20 |
| 21 | 22<br>POST-SEASON<br>TOURNAMENT<br>(AWAY) | 23 | 24 | 25 | 26 | 27 |
| 28 | 29<br>Strength<br>Training<br>Total Body | 30<br>Agility Drills<br>Plyometric<br>Drills | 31 | | | |
| | | | | | | |

# April

## Women's Basketball: Off-Season Training

| SUNDAY | MONDAY | TUESDAY | WEDNESDAY | THURSDAY | FRIDAY | SATURDAY |
|---|---|---|---|---|---|---|
| | | | | **1**<br>3:00 PM:<br>Strength Training<br>Total Body | **2**<br>Agility Drills<br>Plyometric<br>Drills | **3** |
| **4** | **5**<br>3:00 PM:<br>Strength Training<br>Total Body | **6**<br>Agility Drills<br>Plyometric<br>Drills | **7** | **8**<br>3:00 PM:<br>Strength Training<br>Total Body | **9**<br>Agility Drills<br>Plyometric<br>Drills | **10** |
| **11**<br>EASTER | **12**<br>3:00 PM:<br>Strength Training<br>Total Body | **13**<br>Agility Drills<br>Plyometric<br>Drills | **14** | **15**<br>3:00 PM:<br>Strength Training<br>Total Body | **16**<br>Agility Drills<br>Plyometric<br>Drills | **17** |
| **18** | **19**<br>3:00 PM:<br>Strength Training<br>Total Body | **20**<br>Agility Drills<br>Plyometric<br>Drills | **21** | **22**<br>3:00 PM:<br>Strength Training<br>Total Body | **23**<br>Agility Drills<br>Plyometric<br>Drills | **24** |
| **25** | **26**<br>3:00 PM:<br>Strength Training<br>Total Body | **27**<br>Agility Drills<br>Plyometric<br>Drills | **28** | **29**<br>3:00 PM:<br>Strength Training<br>Total Body | **30**<br>Agility Drills<br>Plyometric<br>Drills | |
| | | | | | | |

# May

## Women's Basketball: Off-Season Training

| SUNDAY | MONDAY | TUESDAY | WEDNESDAY | THURSDAY | FRIDAY | SATURDAY |
|---|---|---|---|---|---|---|
| | | | | | | 1 |
| 2 | 3<br>3:00 PM:<br>Strength Training<br>Total Body | 4 | 5 | 6<br>3:00 PM:<br>Strength Training<br>Total Body | 7 | 8 |
| 9 | 10<br>FINAL EXAMS<br>Strength<br>Training (opt.) | 11<br>FINAL EXAMS | 12<br>FINAL EXAMS | 13<br>FINAL EXAMS<br>Strength<br>Training (opt.) | 14<br>FINAL EXAMS | 15 |
| 16 | 17<br>SUMMER<br>BREAK BEGINS | 18 | 19 | 20 | 21 | 22 |
| 23 | 24 | 25 | 26 | 27 | 28 | 29 |
| 30 | 31 | | | | | |

# June

## Women's Basketball: In/Off-Season Training

| SUNDAY | MONDAY | TUESDAY | WEDNESDAY | THURSDAY | FRIDAY | SATURDAY |
|---|---|---|---|---|---|---|
| | | 1<br>Aerobic<br>Conditioning<br>(20:00) | 2<br>Strength<br>Training<br>Upper Body | 3<br>Aerobic<br>Conditioning<br>(20:00) | 4<br>Strength<br>Training<br>Lower Body | 5<br>Aerobic<br>Conditioning<br>(20:00) |
| 6 | 7<br>Strength<br>Training<br>Upper Body | 8<br>Aerobic<br>Conditioning<br>(22:00) | 9<br>Strength<br>Training<br>Lower Body | 10<br>Aerobic<br>Conditioning<br>(22:00) | 11<br>Strength<br>Training<br>Upper Body | 12<br>Aerobic<br>Conditioning<br>(22:00) |
| 13 | 14<br>Strength<br>Training<br>Lower Body | 15<br>Aerobic<br>Conditioning<br>(24:00) | 16<br>Strength<br>Training<br>Upper Body | 17<br>Aerobic<br>Conditioning<br>(24:00) | 18<br>Strength<br>Training<br>Lower Body | 19<br>Aerobic<br>Conditioning<br>(24:00) |
| 20 | 21<br>Strength<br>Training<br>Upper Body | 22<br>Aerobic<br>Conditioning<br>(26:00) | 23<br>Strength<br>Training<br>Lower Body | 24<br>Aerobic<br>Conditioning<br>(26:00) | 25<br>Strength<br>Training<br>Upper Body | 26<br>Aerobic<br>Conditioning<br>(26:00) |
| 27 | 28<br>Strength<br>Training<br>Lower Body | 29<br>Aerobic<br>Conditioning<br>(28:00) | 30<br>Strength<br>Training<br>Upper Body | | | |
| | | | | | | |

# July
## Women's Basketball: In/Off-Season Training

| SUNDAY | MONDAY | TUESDAY | WEDNESDAY | THURSDAY | FRIDAY | SATURDAY |
|---|---|---|---|---|---|---|
| | | | | 1<br>Aerobic<br>Conditioning<br>(28:00) | 2<br>Strength<br>Training<br>Lower Body | 3<br>Aerobic<br>Conditioning<br>(28:00) |
| 4<br>Aerobic<br>Conditioning<br>(30:00) | 5<br>Strength<br>Training<br>Upper Body | 6<br>Aerobic<br>Conditioning<br>(30:00) | 7<br>Strength<br>Training<br>Lower Body | 8<br>Aerobic<br>Conditioning<br>(30:00) | 9<br>Strength<br>Training<br>Upper Body | 10<br>Aerobic<br>Conditioning<br>(30:00) |
| 11<br>Aerobic<br>Conditioning<br>(30:00) | 12<br>Strength<br>Training<br>Lower Body | 13<br>Aerobic<br>Conditioning<br>(30:00) | 14<br>Strength<br>Training<br>Upper Body | 15<br>Aerobic<br>Conditioning<br>(30:00) | 16<br>Strength<br>Training<br>Lower Body | 17<br>Aerobic<br>Conditioning<br>(30:00) |
| 18<br>Aerobic<br>Conditioning<br>(30:00) | 19<br>Strength<br>Training<br>Upper Body | 20<br>Aerobic<br>Conditioning<br>(30:00) | 21<br>Strength<br>Training<br>Lower Body | 22<br>Aerobic<br>Conditioning<br>(30:00) | 23<br>Strength<br>Training<br>Upper Body | 24<br>Aerobic<br>Conditioning<br>(30:00) |
| 25<br>Aerobic<br>Conditioning<br>(30:00) | 26<br>Strength<br>Training<br>Lower Body | 27<br>Aerobic<br>Conditioning<br>(30:00) | 28<br>Strength<br>Training<br>Upper Body | 29<br>Aerobic<br>Conditioning<br>(30:00) | 30<br>Strength<br>Training<br>Lower Body | 31<br>Aerobic<br>Conditioning<br>(30:00) |
| | | | | | | |

# 12

# Conditioning for a Purpose

*John Rinaldo, B.S.*

One of the most important – if not *the* most important – components of any athlete's year-round training regimen is conditioning. An athlete's commitment to conditioning will ultimately determine her physiological performance in the athletic arena. It will also be a determining factor for reducing sport-sustained injuries and, without question, can affect the overall outcome of any athletic event.

In order to fully understand the significance of any conditioning program, it's necessary to be cognizant of the energy systems within the body that serve as the basis for exercise/activity. Furthermore, it's important to understand the types of training that are available and the differences among those types along with the benefits that can be obtained from implementing a conditioning program.

## THE ENERGY SYSTEMS

When training for – and competing in – athletic activities, coaches and athletes should be aware of the energy systems that are utilized. A healthier understanding of the underlying mechanics of these energy systems will allow individuals to make the right choices when deciding upon what kind of training program to adopt for a particular sport or activity.

The two types of systems that the body relies upon for the production of energy are derived from anaerobic and aerobic metabolism. The main difference between the two is simple: Anaerobic metabolism doesn't require the presence of oxygen to function whereas aerobic metabolism does. The following is a brief description of the basic dynamics of the anaerobic and aerobic systems:

### The Anaerobic Systems

The short-term energy systems (or pathways) that the body uses during intense exercise/activity are anaerobic. Generally, the exercise-science community considers the time parameters of anaerobic metabolism to range from the early seconds of exercise/activity to approximately three minutes. This means that anaerobic metabolism is mainly used when putting the shot, doing a back flip, legging out a double, sprinting 400 meters as fast as possible and skating a two-minute shift on the ice. It's essential to understand that anaerobic metabolism is also used any time that an athlete starts an exercise/activity then stops and starts again. So anaerobic metabolism is the primary mechanism that a

**Strength training can produce more of an anaerobic effect by decreasing the recovery interval between sets. (Photo by Pete Silletti)**

basketball player uses during a game because of the start/stop pattern of play.

Anaerobic metabolism has two systems that are independent of one another yet connected by the component of time: the ATP-PC System and the Lactic Acid System. The processes that these two systems undertake in the body are markedly different. But they both yield the same result: the reconstruction of a high-energy compound known as adenosine triphosphate (ATP). When the bonds of ATP are broken, energy is released. The energy systems are used to rebuild the bonds so that ATP can be reused over and over again.

### The ATP-PC System

The anaerobic pathway that's used for brief efforts of the highest intensity is the ATP-PC System. This system relies upon stores of phosphocreatine (PC) as its primary source of fuel. Depending upon the amount of PC that's available in the muscle tissue, the system generally operates for no more than about 30 seconds of intense exercise/activity. Since some individuals have higher amounts of PC than others, the time limit of this system can vary slightly. Nevertheless, the ATP-PC System is the primary energy source that's used during very brief but intense efforts such as performing a 40-yard dash, doing a brief agility drill, throwing a javelin and swinging a softball bat.

### The Lactic Acid System

If the exercise/activity continues beyond about 30 seconds, the anaerobic pathway segues into the Lactic Acid (LA) System. This system relies upon the body's stores of muscle glycogen (carbohydrate) as its primary fuel source (in contrast to the PC that's utilized by the ATP-PC System). The onset of the LA System begins when the body's PC is depleted and no longer available as a fuel. In this system, glycogen is used to rebuild ATP. This metabolic reaction produces lactic acid as a byproduct (which is where the name of the system is derived). The LA System is the primary source of energy that's used during intense efforts that last between about 30 - 180 seconds such as swimming 100 yards, cycling one-half mile and rowing 500 meters (all done as fast as possible) or the start/stop play that's intrinsic to a rugby game.

### The Aerobic System

Recall that the ATP-PC and LA Systems rely upon PC and carbohydrate as their energy sources, respectively. Unlike the anaerobic systems, the Aerobic

System – often referred to as "oxidative metabolism" – depends upon the metabolism of fat as well as carbohydrate to provide energy. Actually, fat is used as the main energy source but it's physiologically impossible to use fat without the presence of carbohydrate. Aerobic metabolism processes the stored fat and enters it into a metabolic chain of events called the "Krebs Cycle" that also uses stored carbohydrate in the course of action.

During activity, aerobic metabolism also serves as the body's long-term energy system. In fact, research has shown that it becomes the body's main energy system after about 15 minutes of continuous activity. The Aerobic System is dominant, then, in sports and activities that are considered to be endurance events. Long-distance efforts – such as cycling, rowing, running and swimming – depend heavily upon the Aerobic System. And although sports and activities that rely upon the anaerobic systems don't often demonstrate the need, there's an aerobic component that can factor into those endeavors as well.

So what happens between the end of anaerobic metabolism and the onset of aerobic metabolism? Well, performing an activity beyond about three minutes requires a blend of anaerobic and aerobic metabolism. As the time of an activity increases, there's a greater reliance upon aerobic metabolism as the primary energy pathway.

## TYPES OF CONDITIONING PROGRAMS

It's been established that the body uses anaerobic and aerobic pathways while training for – and performing in – athletic activities. Concurrently, there are two main types of conditioning programs that can target each of the energy systems in order to prepare for those activities. Based upon the metabolic processes that are involved, these programs are aptly labeled "aerobic" and "anaerobic" conditioning.

### Anaerobic Conditioning

Involvement in any type of anaerobic conditioning (or anaerobic training) can yield a variety of results depending upon an athlete's genetics, lifestyle and nutritional habits. However, research has shown that these programs can decrease body fat, increase muscle mass, muscle strength, resting metabolism and bone density and improve athletic performance, speed and reaction time.

For anaerobic conditioning to be effective, a program must be designed and developed in such a way that it allows the body to utilize anaerobic metabolism for the production of energy. This can be accomplished through several different methods of training. Remember, anaerobic metabolism is primarily used at the onset of intense exercise/activity and continues up to approximately three minutes.

### Components of Anaerobic Conditioning

Before undertaking or designing any anaerobic-conditioning programs, four components (or variables) that are an integral part of any anaerobic protocol must be understood: duration, intensity, frequency and work:rest ratio.

1. Duration. Research has shown that the entire time frame for an anaerobic workout shouldn't exceed about 60 minutes. This is because the body's glycogen stores – which are the primary source of fuel during long-term anaerobic work – are exhausted after about an hour of intense exercise/activity.

   The duration of an anaerobic workout has two considerations: the length of the work interval and the length of the rest/recovery interval that's taken between work intervals. Science has indicated that there's a desired relationship or "ratio" between the work and rest intervals. The work:rest ratio is dependant upon the duration of the work that's performed. It will be discussed later in this section in greater detail.

2. Intensity. For an athlete to obtain any type of anaerobic benefit, the intensity of the anaerobic workout must surpass a certain threshold. During anaerobic conditioning, the intensity (speed) should be sufficiently high to elicit an increase in heart rate. Specifically, she should be training at about 75 - 100% of her maximum heart rate. An athlete's age-predicted maximum heart rate can be determined by using the equation "220 - age." As an example, a 20-year-old athlete would have a predicted maximum heart rate of 200 beats per minute [220 - 20 = 200]. This number would then be multiplied by 75 - 100%. In this instance, an appropriate training range would be about 150 - 200 beats per minute [0.75 x 200 = 150; 1.00 x 200 = 200]. To satisfy this aspect when training, all efforts should be done using about 75% of maximum speed or more. In order to elicit an anaerobic effect from sprint training, then, an athlete would need to run the prescribed distances at roughly 75 - 100% of maximum speed.

   One final note about anaerobic conditioning: The goal isn't to train specifically for speed. Instead, it's to produce a tolerance for lactic acid while performing at higher speeds that can be sustained while using lower recovery intervals.

3. Frequency. Because of the intensity and difficulty that are associated with anaerobic training, a recovery period of about 48 - 72 hours should be allocated between workouts. This period of time will allow for the joints (muscles/tendons) to recover. So in effect, anaerobic workouts should be scheduled 2 - 3 times a week. Using a frequency of training that's greater than three workouts per week may result in overtraining and the conditions that are associated with it. Symptoms of overtraining have been well documented and include insomnia, diarrhea, joint pain, fatigue, loss of appetite and susceptibility to upper-respiratory infections.

4. Work:Rest Ratio. In order to gauge progress and provide athletes with a systematic mechanism of recovery, appropriate work:rest ratios must be prescribed and utilized. For every period of work there needs to be an appropriate period of rest that permits an athlete to recover so that she can produce a subsequent amount of comparable work at a high intensity. These ratios can

be manipulated based upon the conditioning level of an athlete. For instance, the work:rest ratio may be reduced – that is, made more difficult – for an athlete who easily completes each work interval in the allotted time. By doing so, this ensures that the athlete will challenge her system to adapt to the imposed demands and have a greater tolerance for anaerobic work. A summary of work:rest ratios is given in Table 12.1.

| WORK TIME (seconds) | WORK:REST RATIO | REST TIME (seconds) |
|---|---|---|
| 0 - 30 | 1:3 | 30 - 90 |
| 30 - 90 | 1:2 | 60 - 180 |
| 90 - 180 | 1:1 | 90 - 180 |

**TABLE 12.1: SUMMARY OF WORK:REST RATIOS**

## Types of Anaerobic Conditioning

Protocols for anaerobic conditioning can fall under a variety of categories including agility training, skill training, strength training and sprint training. Here's a brief breakdown of how anaerobic training can be incorporated into each of these four categories.

1. Agility Training. Activities that require short bursts of speed or changes of direction can be categorized as agility training. These include performing dot drills, agility ladders and cone drills and jumping rope. Such drills can become part of an anaerobic workout by adhering to appropriate work:rest ratios.

2. Skill Training. Included in skill training are passing a basketball, throwing a softball, hitting a golf ball and shooting a hockey puck. These and other skills can be integrated into an anaerobic workout by dividing the training time into segments while requiring an athlete to perform each skill at a high level of intensity and then providing appropriate rest intervals to allow for recovery. If skill training is incorporated into anaerobic workouts, a caveat is to ensure that an athlete performs the skill with a level of intensity that's high enough to promote improvements.

3. Strength Training. Often referred to as "weight training," strength training can also provide a workout medium that can be integrated into anaerobic conditioning. Usually, strength-training programs – which are anaerobic by nature – stress long periods of relief to ensure that an athlete receives a certain amount of recovery. But strength training can produce more of an anaerobic effect by decreasing the recovery interval between sets. This stimulus can produce results that would be anticipated from typical strength training – namely improvements in muscular strength and, in the case of some females, muscular size (hypertrophy) – as well as benefits that are similar to traditional anaerobic training.

4. Sprint Training. By far, the least complicated activity that can be incorporated into an anaerobic workout is sprint training. Running at high speeds produces large levels of lactic acid that contribute to an anaerobic effect. Also, running speed can be manipulated by enforcing the time parameters for specific distances. For example, how hard an athlete needs to train can be stipulated by setting requirements of a 25-second work interval and a 75-second recovery interval for several consecutive 220-yard sprints thereby ensuring adequate workout intensity. Additionally, sprint training can be applied to workouts in the pool along with different exercise modalities (such as rowing and cycling) and a variety of cardiovascular equipment (such as stairclimbers/steppers, elliptical machines and stationary cycles).

## Aerobic Conditioning

Similar to anaerobic conditioning, aerobic conditioning (or aerobic training) can yield a variety of results depending upon an athlete's genetics, lifestyle and nutritional habits. Research, however, has shown that aerobic conditioning also can improve the cardiovascular system (through increases in oxygen consumption), reduce body fat and cholesterol, improve recovery from anaerobic training/work and decrease mental fatigue.

For aerobic conditioning to be effective, a program must be designed and developed in such a way that it allows the body to utilize aerobic metabolism for the production of energy. This can be accomplished through several different methods of training. Remember, aerobic metabolism is primarily used after about 15 minutes of continuous exercise/activity.

## Components of Aerobic Conditioning

Before undertaking or designing any aerobic-conditioning programs, three components (or variables) that are an integral part of any aerobic protocol must be understood: duration, intensity and frequency.

1. Duration. An aerobic workout should involve at least 15 minutes of continuous activity. In the case of endurance athletes, the duration can progress sometimes to an hour or more. Again, remember that oxidative metabolism doesn't predominate until after prolonged activity.

2. Intensity. For an athlete to obtain any type of aerobic benefit, the intensity of the aerobic workout must surpass a certain threshold. Research has determined that the training range should be about 60 - 90% of an individual's maximum heart rate. As previously noted, the age-predicted maximum heart rate of a 20-year-old athlete is 200 beats per minute. Here, an appropriate training range would be about 120 - 180 beats per minute [0.60 x 200 = 120; 0.90 x 200 = 180].

It's important to note that certain benefits are dependant upon the intensity of the training. In other words, training with different intensities will produce different results. Training at lower heart rates – about 60 - 75% of maximum heart rate – has been shown to produce more peripheral responses in the cardiovascular system such as an increased number of capillaries and decreased levels of fat and cholesterol; training at higher heart rates – about 75 - 90% of maximum heart rate – has been shown to produce more central benefits in the cardiovascular system such as an improved cardiac output, increased ventilation and oxygen consumption and hypertrophy of cardiac tissue.

3. Frequency. In contrast to the frequency requirements of anaerobic conditioning, workouts for aerobic conditioning can be performed on consecutive days – even up to seven days per week. In some instances, sessions can be done more than once a day. However, it's still important to monitor an athlete's progress . . . or lack thereof. Undertrained athletes can become overtrained if they attempt to do too much too soon. And frequent bouts of training that utilize many of the same muscles and joints may result in the same symptoms of overtraining that are associated with anaerobic exercise/activity.

## Types of Aerobic Conditioning

Depending upon the training scenario, there are many common – or "traditional" – activities for aerobic conditioning that can be done without the use of equipment. Activities that don't require equipment – such as running, walking and swimming – can be performed indoors or outdoors. The drawbacks of doing these activities outdoors are, of course, inclement/harsh weather and environmental conditions. For instance, an athlete who lives in Maine could subject herself to harsh conditions by running outdoors in the middle of the winter; an athlete who lives in Florida could subject herself to a dangerous environment by swimming in the coastal waters.

In addition, there are a multitude of activities for aerobic conditioning that can be done with equipment. With the technology that's available in today's market, there are many pieces of exercise equipment that have been developed primarily for aerobic use. This equipment can be stationary (such as cycles, stairclimbers/steppers, elliptical machines, treadmills and rowing ergometers) or non-stationary (such as outdoor cycles, canoes and any type of boat that can be rowed).

## INTERDEPENDENT RELATIONSHIPS BETWEEN CONDITIONING PROGRAMS

Although anaerobic and aerobic conditioning may seem mutually exclusive, they aren't. The benefits derived from aerobic conditioning have a direct impact upon anaerobic conditioning and vice versa. It should be understood that aerobic conditioning increases an athlete's ability to recover during anaerobic work. As an example, aerobic conditioning allows a hockey player's heart rate to return to normal more quickly after skating an intense two-minute shift on the ice. On the other hand, anaerobic conditioning can affect an athlete's performance during an activity that relies predominantly on aerobic conditioning. As an example, a long-distance runner can improve her sprinting speed at the end of a race by doing anaerobic conditioning to supplement her aerobic conditioning. The fact is that there's an interdependent relationship between the aerobic and anaerobic energy systems that influences the same relationship between aerobic and anaerobic conditioning.

## GENDER ISSUES AND CONDITIONING

There are three gender-specific issues of which female athletes should be aware as they partake in any type of aerobic or anaerobic conditioning: the Q-angle of the hip and knee as it relates to the female skeletal structure; the menstrual cycle of the reproductive organs; and thermal stress associated with heat production during exercise/activity.

### Q Angle

Measuring the difference in angles between the knee and two different points in the hip area determines the Q-angle. Genetically, women have a larger Q-angle than men – 15 degrees to 10, respectively. Female athletes who exhibit a Q-angle greater than 20 degrees have a greater potential for various maladies including patella-tracking problems in the knee.

### Menstruation

Intense exercise/activity has proven to cause an irregularity in – or a cessation of – the menstrual cycle. Some research has shown that this could provide a health benefit by lowering the risk of cancer in the breasts and reproductive organs. In addition, other research has suggested that the different phases of the menstrual process may be factors in sports performance. Nonetheless, this has yet to be determined conclusively.

### Thermal Stress

There are varying reports that indicate gender can affect the amount of heat stress produced during exercise/activity. Early studies showed that women couldn't tolerate the production of exercise-induced heat as well as their male counterparts. In contrast, recent studies indicate that male and female athletes can tolerate equally the heat stress that's associated with exercise. While this may be valid, there are several surefire ways for an athlete to reduce the effects of thermal stress such as keeping well ventilated, staying hydrated, replacing lost electrolytes during exercise/activity and avoiding the use of diuretics.

## CONCLUDING REMARKS

For athletes to achieve success in any given endeavor, it's paramount that they and their respective trainers understand the mechanisms and benefits of anaerobic and aerobic conditioning. Far too often, these areas of training are neglected – aerobic conditioning in particular – only to witness an athlete fall short of a team's desired aspirations. In order to achieve success, it then rests upon the knowledge of well-prepared coaches to educate and train each athlete so that she can compete at her highest level.

# Appendix: 24 Interval Workouts

# SHUTTLE RUN INTERVALS

## VENUE: *BASKETBALL COURT*
## DISTANCE: *63-yard Long Shuttle*

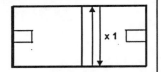

| LEVEL | REPS (TOTAL DISTANCE) | % SPEED | W:R RATIO | TARGET TIME | RECOVERY TIME | | RUN PACE @ 32 YARDS |
|---|---|---|---|---|---|---|---|
| 1 | 8 (504 yards) | 77.5 | 1:4.5 | GP1 = 0:11.0 GP2 = 0:11.5 GP3 = 0:12.5 GP4 = 0:13.0 | 0:48 0:52 0:55 0:59 | (1 = 0:53) [2 = 0:41] {3 = 0:30} | 0:05.50 0:05.75 0:06.25 0:06.50 |
| 2 | 12 (756 yards) | 82.5 | 1:4 | GP1 = 0:10.5 GP2 = 0:11.0 GP3 = 0:12.0 GP4 = 0:12.5 | 0:41 0:44 0:47 0:50 | (1 = 0:46) [2 = 0:34] {3 = 0:23} | 0:05.25 0:05.50 0:06.00 0:06.25 |
| 3 | 16 (1,008 yards) | 87.5 | 1:3.5 | GP1 = 0:10.0 GP2 = 0:10.5 GP3 = 0: 11.5 GP4 = 0:12.0 | 0:35 0:37 0:40 0:42 | (1 = 0:38) [2 = 0:27] {3 = 0:16} | 0:05.00 0:05.25 0:05.75 0:06.00 |
| 4 | 20 (1,260 yards) | 92.5 | 1:3 | GP1 = 0:09.5 GP2 = 0:10.0 GP3 = 0:11.0 GP4 = 0:11.5 | 0:29 0:31 0:33 0:35 | (1 = 0:32) [2 = 0:21] {3 = 0:11} | 0:04.75 0:05.00 0:05.50 0:05.75 |

## VENUE: *BASKETBALL COURT*
## DISTANCE: *33-yard Side Shuttle*

| LEVEL | REPS (TOTAL DISTANCE) | % SPEED | W:R RATIO | TARGET TIME | RECOVERY TIME | | RUN PACE |
|---|---|---|---|---|---|---|---|
| 1 | 10 (330 yards) | 80 | 1:5 | GP1 = 0:06.1 GP2 = 0:06.5 GP3 = 0:06.9 GP4 = 0:07.3 | 0:30 0:33 0:34 0:36 | (1 = 0:33) [2 = 0:27] {3 = 0:20} | |
| 2 | 15 (495 yards) | 85 | 1:4.5 | GP1 = 0:05.9 GP2 = 0:06.3 GP3 = 0:06.7 GP4 = 0:07.0 | 0:27 0:28 0:30 0:32 | (1 = 0:29) [2 = 0:23] {3 = 0:16} | N.A. |
| 3 | 20 (660 yards) | 90 | 1:4 | GP1 = 0:05.7 GP2 = 0:06.1 GP3 = 0:06.4 GP4 = 0:06.8 | 0:23 0:24 0:26 0:37 | (1 = 0:25) [2 = 0:19] {3 = 0:12} | |
| 4 | 25 (825 yards) | 95 | 1:3.5 | GP1 = 0:05.5 GP2 = 0:05.8 GP3 = 0:06.2 GP4 = 0:06.5 | 0:19 0:20 0:22 0:23 | (1 = 0:21) [2 = 0:15] {3 = 0:09} | |

# SHUTTLE RUN INTERVALS

**VENUE: BASKETBALL COURT**

**DISTANCE: 125-yard Long Shuttle**

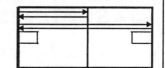

| LEVEL | REPS (TOTAL DISTANCE) | % SPEED | W:R RATIO | TARGET TIME | RECOVERY TIME | | RUN PACE @ 63 YARDS |
|---|---|---|---|---|---|---|---|
| **1** | **6** (750 yards) | 75 | 1:4.25 | GP1 = 0:23.0<br>GP2 = 0:24.5<br>GP3 = 0:26.0<br>GP4 = 0:27.5 | 1:37<br>1:44<br>1:51<br>1:57 | (1 = 1:47)<br>[2 = 1:22]<br>{3 = 0:57} | 0:11.50<br>0:12.25<br>0:13.00<br>0:13.75 |
| **2** | **8** (1,000 yards) | 80 | 1:3.75 | GP1 = 0:22.0<br>GP2 = 0:23.5<br>GP3 = 0:25.0<br>GP4 = 0:26.5 | 1:23<br>1:29<br>1:34<br>1:40 | (1 = 1:31)<br>[2 = 1:07]<br>{3 = 0:43} | 0:11.00<br>0:11.75<br>0:12.50<br>0:13.25 |
| **3** | **12** (1,500 yards) | 85 | 1:3.25 | GP1 = 0:21.5<br>GP2 = 0:23.0<br>GP3 = 0:24.0<br>GP4 = 0:25.5 | 1:10<br>1:14<br>1:19<br>1:24 | (1 = 1:16)<br>[2 = 0:53]<br>{3 = 0:29} | 0:10.75<br>0:11.50<br>0:12.00<br>0:12.75 |
| **4** | **14** (1,750 yards) | 90 | 1:2.75 | GP1 = 0:20.5<br>GP2 = 0:22.0<br>GP3 = 0:23.5<br>GP4 = 0:24.5 | 0:57<br>1:00<br>1:04<br>1:08 | (1 = 1:02)<br>[2 = 0:40]<br>{3 = 0:17} | 0:10.25<br>0:11.00<br>0:11.75<br>0:12.25 |

**VENUE: BASKETBALL COURT**

**DISTANCE: 94-yard Long Shuttle**

| LEVEL | REPS (TOTAL DISTANCE) | % SPEED | W:R RATIO | TARGET TIME | RECOVERY TIME | | RUN PACE @ 47 YARDS |
|---|---|---|---|---|---|---|---|
| **1** | **6** (564 yards) | 77.5 | 1:4.5 | GP1 = 0:18.0<br>GP2 = 0:19.0<br>GP3 = 0:20.0<br>GP4 = 0:21.0 | 1:21<br>1:26<br>1:31<br>1:36 | (1 = 1:28)<br>[2 = 1:09]<br>{3 = 0:49} | 0:09.00<br>0:09.50<br>0:10.00<br>0:10.50 |
| **2** | **10** (940 yards) | 82.5 | 1:4 | GP1 = 0:17.5<br>GP2 = 0:18.5<br>GP3 = 0:19.5<br>GP4 = 0:20.5 | 1:09<br>1:14<br>1:18<br>1:22 | (1 = 1:16)<br>[2 = 0:57]<br>{3 = 0:38} | 0:08.75<br>0:09.25<br>0:09.75<br>0:10.25 |
| **3** | **14** (1,316 yards) | 87.5 | 1:3.5 | GP1 = 0:16.5<br>GP2 = 0:18.0<br>GP3 = 0:19.0<br>GP4 = 0:20.0 | 0:58<br>1:02<br>1:06<br>1:10 | (1 = 1:04)<br>[2 = 0:46]<br>{3 = 0:27} | 0:08.25<br>0:09.00<br>0:09.50<br>0:10.00 |
| **4** | **18** (1,692 yards) | 92.5 | 1:3 | GP1 = 0:16.0<br>GP2 = 0:17.0<br>GP3 = 0:18.0<br>GP4 = 0:19.0 | 0:48<br>0:51<br>0:54<br>0:58 | (1 = 0:53)<br>[2 = 0:35]<br>{3 = 0:18} | 0:08.00<br>0:08.50<br>0:09.00<br>0:09.50 |

# SHORT INTERVALS

**VENUE:** **SOFTBALL FIELD**

**DISTANCE:** **140 yards** *(down and back = 70 yards)*

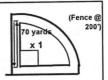

| LEVEL | REPS (TOTAL DISTANCE) | % SPEED | W:R RATIO | TARGET E18TIME | RECOVERY TIME | | RUN PACE @ 70 YARDS |
|---|---|---|---|---|---|---|---|
| 1 | 6 (840 yards) | 75 | 1:4.25 | GP1 = 0:23.0 GP2 = 0:24.5 GP3 = 0:26.0 GP4 = 0:28.0 | 1:51 1:59 2:08 2:16 | (1 = 2:04) [2 = 1:35] {3 = 1:06} | 0:12.00 0:12.25 0:13.00 0:14.00 |
| 2 | 8 (1,120 yards) | 80 | 1:3.75 | GP1 = 0:22.0 GP2 = 0:23.5 GP3 = 0:25.0 GP4 = 0:27.0 | 1:34 1:41 1:49 1:53 | (1 = 1:45) [2 = 1:17] {3 = 0:49} | 0:11.00 0:11.75 0:12.50 0:13.50 |
| 3 | 12 (1,680 yards) | 85 | 1:3.25 | GP1 = 0:21.0 GP2 = 0:23.0 GP3 = 0:24.0 GP4 = 0:26.0 | 1:18 1:25 1:31 1:34 | (1 = 1:28) [2 = 1:01] {3 = 0:34} | 0:10.50 0:11.50 0:12.00 0:13.00 |
| 4 | 14 (1,960 yards) | 90 | 1:2.75 | GP1 = 0:20.0 GP2 = 0:22.0 GP3 = 0:23.0 GP4 = 0:25.0 | 1:03 1:09 1:14 1:17 | (1 = 1:12) [2 = 0:46] {3 = 0:20} | 0:10.00 0:11.00 0:11.50 0:12.50 |

**VENUE:** **SOFTBALL FIELD**

**DISTANCE:** **120 yards** *(3B line to 1B line on the warning track)*

| LEVEL | REPS (TOTAL DISTANCE) | % SPEED | W:R RATIO | TARGET TIME | RECOVERY TIME | | RUN PACE |
|---|---|---|---|---|---|---|---|
| 1 | 6 (720 yards) | 75 | 1:4.25 | GP1 = 0:18.5 GP2 = 0:20.0 GP3 = 0:21.5 GP4 = 0:23.0 | 1:18 1:25 1:31 1:37 | (1 = 1:28) [2 = 1:07] {3 = 0:46} | |
| 2 | 8 (960 yards) | 80 | 1:3.75 | GP1 = 0:17.5 GP2 = 0:19.0 GP3 = 0:20.5 GP4 = 0:22.0 | 1:06 1:12 1:17 1:22 | (1 = 1:14) [2 = 0:54] {3 = 0:35} | N.A. |
| 3 | 12 (1,440 yards) | 85 | 1:3.25 | GP1 = 0:17.0 GP2 = 0:18.5 GP3 = 0:20.0 GP4 = 0:21.0 | 0:55 0:59 1:04 1:08 | (1 = 1:02) [2 = 0:43] {3 = 0:24} | |
| 4 | 14 (1,680 yards) | 90 | 1:2.75 | GP1 = 0:16.0 GP2 = 0:17.5 GP3 = 0:19.0 GP4 = 0:20.0 | 0:45 0:48 0:52 0:55 | (1 = 0:50) [2 = 0:32] {3 = 0:14} | |

# LONG INTERVALS

**VENUE:** *SOFTBALL FIELD*

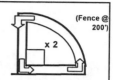

(Fence @ 200')

**DISTANCE:** **530 yards** *(2 laps around the field on the warning track)*

| LEVEL | REPS (TOTAL DISTANCE) | % SPEED | W:R RATIO | TARGET TIME | RECOVERY TIME | | RUN PACE @ 265 YARDS |
|---|---|---|---|---|---|---|---|
| 1 | 3 (1,590 yards) | 40 | 1:2.75 | GP1 = 1:43<br>GP2 = 1:52<br>GP3 = 2:00<br>GP4 = 2:09 | 4:43<br>5:08<br>5:30<br>5:55 | (1 = 5:19)<br>[2 = 3:23]<br>{3 = 1:27} | 0:52<br>0:56<br>1:00<br>1:05 |
| 2 | 4 (2,120 yards) | 50 | 1:2.25 | GP1 = 1:37<br>GP2 = 1:45<br>GP3 = 1:53<br>GP4 = 2:01 | 3:38<br>3:56<br>4:14<br>4:32 | (1 = 4:05)<br>[2 = 2:16]<br>{3 = 0:27} | 0:49<br>0:53<br>0:57<br>1:01 |
| 3 | 5 (2,650 yards) | 60 | 1:1.75 | GP1 = 1:30<br>GP2 = 1:38<br>GP3 = 1:45<br>GP4 = 1:53 | 2:38<br>2:52<br>3:04<br>3:18 | (1 = 2:58)<br>[2 = 1:16] | 0:45<br>0:49<br>0:53<br>0:57 |
| 4 | 6 (3,180 yards) | 70 | 1:1.25 | GP1 = 1:24<br>GP2 = 1:31<br>GP3 = 1:38<br>GP4 = 1:45 | 1:45<br>1:54<br>2:02<br>2:11 | (1 = 1:58)<br>[2 = 0:24] | 0:42<br>0:46<br>0:49<br>0:53 |

**VENUE:** *SOFTBALL FIELD*

(Fence @ 200')

**DISTANCE:** **265 yards** *(1 lap around the field on the warning track)*

| LEVEL | REPS (TOTAL DISTANCE) | % SPEED | W:R RATIO | TARGET TIME | RECOVERY TIME | | RUN PACE |
|---|---|---|---|---|---|---|---|
| 1 | 4 (1,060 yards) | 60.0 | 1:3.5 | GP1 = 0:45<br>GP2 = 0:50<br>GP3 = 0:53<br>GP4 = 0:57 | 2:39<br>2:52<br>3:05<br>3:18 | (1 = 2:59)<br>[2 = 2:08]<br>{3 = 1:17} | |
| 2 | 6 (1,590 yards) | 67.5 | 1:3 | GP1 = 0:43<br>GP2 = 0:47<br>GP3 = 0:50<br>GP4 = 0:54 | 2:09<br>2:20<br>2:30<br>2:41 | (1 = 2:25)<br>[2 = 1:37]<br>{3 = 0:48} | N.A. |
| 3 | 8 (2,120 yards) | 75.0 | 1:2.5 | GP1 = 0:41<br>GP2 = 0:44<br>GP3 = 0:47<br>GP4 = 0:51 | 1:42<br>1:50<br>1:58<br>2:06 | (1 = 1:54)<br>[2 = 1:08]<br>{3 = 0:23} | |
| 4 | 10 (2,650 yards) | 82.5 | 1:2 | GP1 = 0:38<br>GP2 = 0:41<br>GP3 = 0:45<br>GP4 = 0:48 | 1:16<br>1:23<br>1:29<br>1:35 | (1 = 1:26)<br>[2 = 0:43]<br>{3 = 0:00} | |

# SHORT INTERVALS

**VENUE:** *SOCCER/FOOTBALL FIELD*

**DISTANCE:** **200 yards** *(100 yards down and back)*

| LEVEL | REPS (TOTAL DISTANCE) | % SPEED | W:R RATIO | TARGET TIME | RECOVERY TIME | | RUN PACE @ 100 YARDS |
|---|---|---|---|---|---|---|---|
| 1 | 5 (1,000 yards) | 65.0 | 1:4 | GP1 = 0:34<br>GP2 = 0:37<br>GP3 = 0:40<br>GP4 = 0:42 | 2:17<br>2:28<br>2:39<br>2:50 | (1 = 2:38)<br>[2 = 1:55]<br>{3 = 1:17} | 0:17<br>0:19<br>0:20<br>0:21 |
| 2 | 7 (1,400 yards) | 72.5 | 1:3.5 | GP1 = 0:33<br>GP2 = 0:35<br>GP3 = 0:37<br>GP4 = 0:40 | 1:54<br>2:02<br>2:12<br>2:20 | (1 = 2:00)<br>[2 = 1:31]<br>{3 = 0:54} | 0:17<br>0:18<br>0:19<br>0:20 |
| 3 | 10 (2,000 yards) | 80 | 1:3 | GP1 = 0:31<br>GP2 = 0:33<br>GP3 = 0:36<br>GP4 = 0:38 | 1:32<br>1:39<br>1:46<br>1:54 | (1 = 1:43)<br>[2 = 1:09]<br>{3 = 0:34} | 0:16<br>0:17<br>0:18<br>0:19 |
| 4 | 12 (2,400 yards) | 87.5 | 1:2.5 | GP1 = 0:29<br>GP2 = 0:31<br>GP3 = 0:33<br>GP4 = 0:36 | 1:12<br>1:18<br>1:23<br>1:29 | (1 = 1:20)<br>[2 = 0:48]<br>{3 = 0:16} | 0:15<br>0:16<br>0:17<br>0:18 |

**VENUE:** *SOCCER/FOOTBALL FIELD*

**DISTANCE:** **100 yards** *(100 yards down field)*

| LEVEL | REPS (TOTAL DISTANCE) | % SPEED | W:R RATIO | TARGET TIME | RECOVERY TIME | | RUN PACE |
|---|---|---|---|---|---|---|---|
| 1 | 8 (800 yards) | 77.5 | 1:4.5 | GP1 = 0:15.0<br>GP2 = 0:16.0<br>GP3 = 0:17.5<br>GP4 = 0:19.0 | 1:07<br>1:13<br>1:19<br>1:24 | (1 = 1:16)<br>[2 = 0:59]<br>{3 = 0:42} | |
| 2 | 10 (1,000 yards) | 82.5 | 1:4 | GP1 = 0:14.5<br>GP2 = 0:15.5<br>GP3 = 0:16.5<br>GP4 = 0:18.0 | 0:58<br>1:02<br>1:07<br>1:12 | (1 = 1:05)<br>[2 = 0:48]<br>{3 = 0:32} | N.A. |
| 3 | 14 (1,400 yards) | 87.5 | 1:3.5 | GP1 = 0:14.0<br>GP2 = 0:15.0<br>GP3 = 0:16.0<br>GP4 = 0:17.0 | 0:48<br>0:52<br>0:56<br>1:00 | (1 = 0:54)<br>[2 = 0:39]<br>{3 = 0:22} | |
| 4 | 16 (1,600 yards) | 92.5 | 1:3 | GP1 = 0:13.0<br>GP2 = 0:14.0<br>GP3 = 0:15.0<br>GP4 = 0:16.5 | 0:40<br>0:43<br>0:46<br>0:49 | (1 = 0:44)<br>[2 = 0:30]<br>{3 = 0:15} | |

# LONG INTERVALS

**VENUE:** *SOCCER/FOOTBALL FIELD*

**DISTANCE:** **680 yards** *(2 laps around 120-yard x 53-yard field)*

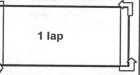

2 laps

| LEVEL | REPS (TOTAL DISTANCE) | % SPEED | W:R RATIO | TARGET TIME | RECOVERY TIME | | RUN PACE @ 340 YARDS |
|---|---|---|---|---|---|---|---|
| 1 | 2 (1,360 yards) | 35 | 1:2.5 | GP1 = 2:17<br>GP2 = 2:29<br>GP3 = 2:40<br>GP4 = 2:51 | 5:42<br>6:13<br>6:40<br>7:08 | (1 = 6:26)<br>[2 = 3:52]<br>{3 = 1:17} | 1:09<br>1:15<br>1:20<br>1:26 |
| 2 | 3 (2,040 yards) | 45 | 1:2 | GP1 = 2:09<br>GP2 = 2:20<br>GP3 = 2:30<br>GP4 = 2:41 | 4:18<br>4:40<br>5:00<br>5:22 | (1 = 4:50)<br>[2 = 2:25]<br>{3 = 0:00} | 1:05<br>1:10<br>1:15<br>1:21 |
| 3 | 4 (2,720 yards) | 55 | 1:1.5 | GP1 = 2:01<br>GP2 = 2:11<br>GP3 = 2:21<br>GP4 = 2:30 | 3:02<br>3:17<br>3:32<br>3:45 | (1 = 3:24)<br>[2 = 1:08] | 1:01<br>1:06<br>1:11<br>1:15 |
| 4 | 5 (3,400 yards) | 65 | 1:1 | GP1 = 1:52<br>GP2 = 2:02<br>GP3 = 2:11<br>GP4 = 2:20 | 1:52<br>2:02<br>2:11<br>2:20 | (1 = 2:07)<br>[2 = 0:00] | 0:56<br>1:10<br>1:06<br>1:10 |

**VENUE:** *SOCCER/FOOTBALL FIELD*

**DISTANCE:** **340 yards** *(1 lap around 120-yard x 53-yard field)*

1 lap

| LEVEL | REPS (TOTAL DISTANCE) | % SPEED | W:R RATIO | TARGET TIME | RECOVERY TIME | | RUN PACE @ 170 YARDS |
|---|---|---|---|---|---|---|---|
| 1 | 4 (1,360 yards) | 50 | 1:3.25 | GP1 = 1:02<br>GP2 = 1:08<br>GP3 = 1:13<br>GP4 = 1:18 | 3:22<br>3:41<br>3:57<br>4:14 | (1 = 3:49)<br>[2 = 2:38]<br>{3 = 1:28} | 0:31<br>0:34<br>0:37<br>0:39 |
| 2 | 5 (1,700 yards) | 60 | 1:2.75 | GP1 = 0:58<br>GP2 = 1:03<br>GP3 = 1:08<br>GP4 = 1:13 | 2:40<br>2:53<br>3:07<br>3:21 | (1 = 3:00)<br>[2 = 1:55]<br>{3 = 0:49} | 0:29<br>0:32<br>0:34<br>0:37 |
| 3 | 7 (2,380 yards) | 70 | 1:2.25 | GP1 = 0:54<br>GP2 = 0:59<br>GP3 = 1:03<br>GP4 = 1:07 | 2:02<br>2:12<br>2:22<br>2:31 | (1 = 2:17)<br>[2 = 1:16]<br>{3 = 0:15} | 0:27<br>0:30<br>0:32<br>0:34 |
| 4 | 8 (2,720 yards) | 80 | 1:1.75 | GP1 = 0:50<br>GP2 = 0:54<br>GP3 = 0:58<br>GP4 = 1:02 | 1:28<br>1:35<br>1:42<br>1:49 | (1 = 1:38)<br>[2 = 0:42] | 0:25<br>0:27<br>0:29<br>0:31 |

# SHORT INTERVALS

**VENUE: *OUTDOOR TRACK***

**DISTANCE: *200 meters*** *(1/2 lap on a 400-meter track)*

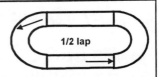

| LEVEL | REPS (TOTAL DISTANCE) | % SPEED | W:R RATIO | TARGET TIME | RECOVERY TIME | | RUN PACE |
|---|---|---|---|---|---|---|---|
| 1 | 4 (872 yards) | 62.5 | 1:3.75 | GP1 = 0:37<br>GP2 = 0:40<br>GP3 = 0:43<br>GP4 = 0:46 | 2:18<br>2:29<br>2:40<br>2:51 | (1 = 2:34)<br>[2 = 1:53]<br>{3 = 1:12} | |
| 2 | 6 (1,308 yards) | 70.0 | 1:3.25 | GP1 = 0:35<br>GP2 = 0:38<br>GP3 = 0:40<br>GP4 = 0:43 | 1:53<br>2:02<br>2:11<br>2:20 | (1 = 2:07)<br>[2 = 1:28]<br>{3 = 0:49} | N.A. |
| 3 | 8 (1,744 yards) | 77.5 | 1:2.75 | GP1 = 0:33<br>GP2 = 0:35<br>GP3 = 0:38<br>GP4 = 0:41 | 1:30<br>1:37<br>1:45<br>1:52 | (1 = 1:41)<br>[2 = 1:04]<br>{3 = 0:28} | |
| 4 | 10 (2,180 yards) | 85.0 | 1:2.25 | GP1 = 0:31<br>GP2 = 0:33<br>GP3 = 0:36<br>GP4 = 0:38 | 1:09<br>1:15<br>1:20<br>1:26 | (1 = 1:18)<br>[2 = 0:43]<br>{3 = 0:09} | |

**VENUE: *OUTDOOR TRACK***

**DISTANCE: *100 meters*** *(100 meters on a 400-meter track)*

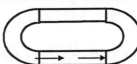

| LEVEL | REPS (TOTAL DISTANCE) | % SPEED | W:R RATIO | TARGET TIME | RECOVERY TIME | | RUN PACE |
|---|---|---|---|---|---|---|---|
| 1 | 8 (872 yards) | 75 | 1:4.25 | GP1 = 0:17.0<br>GP2 = 0:18.0<br>GP3 = 0:19.5<br>GP4 = 0:21.0 | 1:11<br>1:17<br>1:22<br>1:28 | (1 = 1:20)<br>[2 = 1:01]<br>{3 = 0:42} | |
| 2 | 10 (1,090 yards) | 80 | 1:3.75 | GP1 = 0:16.0<br>GP2 = 0:17.0<br>GP3 = 0:18.0<br>GP4 = 0:19.0 | 1:00<br>1:05<br>1:10<br>1:15 | (1 = 1:06)<br>[2 = 0:49]<br>{3 = 0:30} | N.A. |
| 3 | 14 (1,526 yards) | 85 | 1:3.25 | GP1 = 0:15.0<br>GP2 = 0:16.0<br>GP3 = 0:17.0<br>GP4 = 0:18.0 | 0:50<br>0:54<br>0:58<br>1:02 | (1 = 0:56)<br>[2 = 0:39]<br>{3 = 0:22} | |
| 4 | 16 (1,744 yards) | 90 | 1:2.75 | GP1 = 0:14.0<br>GP2 = 0:15.0<br>GP3 = 0:16.0<br>GP4 = 0:17.0 | 0:40<br>0:44<br>0:47<br>0:50 | (1 = 0:45)<br>[2 = 0:29]<br>{3 = 0:12} | |

# LONG INTERVALS

**VENUE: OUTDOOR TRACK**

**DISTANCE: 800 meters** *(2 laps around a 400-meter track)*

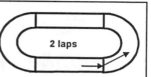

| LEVEL | REPS<br>(TOTAL DISTANCE) | %<br>SPEED | W:R<br>RATIO | TARGET TIME | RECOVERY TIME | | RUN PACE<br>@ 400 METERS |
|---|---|---|---|---|---|---|---|
| **1** | **2**<br>(1,744 yards) | 25 | 1:2 | GP1 = 3:07<br>GP2 = 3:22<br>GP3 = 3:37<br>GP4 = 3:53 | 6:14<br>6:44<br>7:14<br>7:46 | (1 = 6:59)<br>[2 = 3:30]<br>{3 = 0:00} | 1:34<br>1:41<br>1:49<br>1:57 |
| **2** | **3**<br>(2,616 yards) | 35 | 1:1.5 | GP1 = 2:56<br>GP2 = 3:11<br>GP3 = 3:25<br>GP4 = 3:39 | 4:24<br>4:46<br>5:07<br>5:28 | (1 = 4:57)<br>[2 = 1:39] | 1:28<br>1:35<br>1:42<br>1:49 |
| **3** | **4**<br>(3,488 yards) | 45 | 1:1 | GP1 = 2:46<br>GP2 = 2:59<br>GP3 = 3:13<br>GP4 = 3:26 | 2:46<br>2:59<br>3:13<br>3:26 | (1 = 3:06)<br>[2 = 0:00] | 1:23<br>1:30<br>1:37<br>1:43 |
| **4** | **5**<br>(4,360 yards) | 55 | 1:0.5 | GP1 = 2:35<br>GP2 = 2:48<br>GP3 = 3:00<br>GP4 = 3:13 | 1:18<br>1:24<br>1:30<br>1:37 | (1 = 1:27) | 1:18<br>1:24<br>1:30<br>1:37 |

**VENUE: OUTDOOR TRACK**

**DISTANCE: 400 meters** *(1 lap around a 400-meter track)*

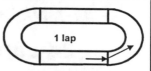

| LEVEL | REPS<br>(TOTAL DISTANCE) | %<br>SPEED | W:R<br>RATIO | TARGET TIME | RECOVERY TIME | | RUN PACE<br>@ 200 METERS |
|---|---|---|---|---|---|---|---|
| **1** | **3**<br>(1,308 yards) | 45 | 1:3 | GP1 = 1:23<br>GP2 = 1:30<br>GP3 = 1:36<br>GP4 = 1:43 | 4:09<br>4:30<br>4:48<br>5:09 | (1 = 4:39)<br>[2 = 3:06]<br>{3 = 1:33} | 0:42<br>0:45<br>0:48<br>0:52 |
| **2** | **4**<br>(1,744 yards) | 55 | 1:2.5 | GP1 = 1:17<br>GP2 = 1:24<br>GP3 = 1:30<br>GP4 = 1:36 | 3:13<br>3:30<br>3:45<br>4:00 | (1 = 3:38)<br>[2 = 2:10]<br>{3 = 0:43} | 0:39<br>0:42<br>0:45<br>0:48 |
| **3** | **6**<br>(2,616 yards) | 65 | 1:2 | GP1 = 1:12<br>GP2 = 1:18<br>GP3 = 1:24<br>GP4 = 1:30 | 2:24<br>2:36<br>2:48<br>3:00 | (1 = 2:42)<br>[2 = 1:21] | 0:36<br>0:39<br>0:42<br>0:45 |
| **4** | **7**<br>(3,052 yards) | 75 | 1:1.5 | GP1 = 1:07<br>GP2 = 1:12<br>GP3 = 1:18<br>GP4 = 1:23 | 1:41<br>1:48<br>1:57<br>2:05 | (1 = 1:53)<br>[2 = 0:38] | 0:34<br>0:36<br>0:39<br>0:42 |

# SHUTTLE RUN INTERVALS

**VENUE: TENNIS COURT**

**DISTANCE: 38-yard Long Shuttle**

| LEVEL | REPS (TOTAL DISTANCE) | % SPEED | W:R RATIO | TARGET TIME | RECOVERY TIME | | RUN PACE |
|---|---|---|---|---|---|---|---|
| 1 | 10 (380 yards) | 80 | 1:5 | GP1 = 0:09.3<br>GP2 = 0:09.8<br>GP3 = 0:10.2<br>GP4 = 0:10.7 | 0:44<br>0:47<br>0:51<br>0:53 | (1 = 0:50)<br>[2 = 0:40]<br>{3 = 0:30} | |
| 2 | 15 (570 yards) | 85 | 1:4.5 | GP1 = 0:09.1<br>GP2 = 0:09.5<br>GP3 = 0:10.0<br>GP4 = 0:10.4 | 0:41<br>0:43<br>0:45<br>0:47 | (1 = 0:44)<br>[2 = 0:34]<br>{3 = 0:24} | N.A. |
| 3 | 20 (760 yards) | 90 | 1:4 | GP1 = 0:08.9<br>GP2 = 0:09.3<br>GP3 = 0:09.7<br>GP4 = 0:10.1 | 0:35<br>0:37<br>0:39<br>0:40 | (1 = 0:38)<br>[2 = 0:29]<br>{3 = 0:19} | |
| 4 | 25 (950 yards) | 95 | 1:3.5 | GP1 = 0:08.6<br>GP2 = 0:09.0<br>GP3 = 0:09.4<br>GP4 = 0:09.8 | 0:30<br>0:32<br>0:33<br>0:34 | (1 = 0:32)<br>[2 = 0:23]<br>{3 = 0:14} | |

**VENUE: TENNIS COURT**

**DISTANCE: 24-yard Side Shuttle**

| LEVEL | REPS (TOTAL DISTANCE) | % SPEED | W:R RATIO | TARGET TIME | RECOVERY TIME | | RUN PACE |
|---|---|---|---|---|---|---|---|
| 1 | 10 (240 yards) | 80 | 1:5 | GP1 = 0:04.8<br>GP2 = 0:05.1<br>GP3 = 0:05.3<br>GP4 = 0:05.6 | 0:24<br>0:25<br>0:27<br>0:28 | (1 = 0:26)<br>[2 = 0:21]<br>{3 = 0:16} | |
| 2 | 15 (360 yards) | 85 | 1:4.5 | GP1 = 0:04.6<br>GP2 = 0:04.9<br>GP3 = 0:05.2<br>GP4 = 0:05.5 | 0:21<br>0:22<br>0:23<br>0:25 | (1 = 0:23)<br>[2 = 0:18]<br>{3 = 0:13} | N.A. |
| 3 | 20 (480 yards) | 90 | 1:4 | GP1 = 0:04.5<br>GP2 = 0:04.8<br>GP3 = 0:05.0<br>GP4 = 0:05.3 | 0:18<br>0:19<br>0:20<br>0:21 | (1 = 0:20)<br>[2 = 0:15]<br>{3 = 0:10} | |
| 4 | 25 (600 yards) | 95 | 1:3.5 | GP1 = 0:04.3<br>GP2 = 0:04.6<br>GP3 = 0:04.8<br>GP4 = 0:05.1 | 0:15<br>0:16<br>0:17<br>0:18 | (1 = 0:17)<br>[2 = 0:12]<br>{3 = 0:07} | |

# SHUTTLE RUN INTERVALS

**VENUE:** *TENNIS COURT*

**DISTANCE:** *104-yard Long Shuttle*

| LEVEL | REPS<br>(TOTAL DISTANCE) | %<br>SPEED | W:R<br>RATIO | TARGET TIME | RECOVERY TIME | | RUN PACE<br>@ 52 YARDS |
|---|---|---|---|---|---|---|---|
| 1 | 8<br>(832 yards) | 75 | 1:4.25 | GP1 = 0:20.0<br>GP2 = 0:21.0<br>GP3 = 0:22.0<br>GP4 = 0:23.5 | 1:24<br>1:29<br>1:35<br>1:40 | (1 = 1:32)<br>[2 = 1:10]<br>{3 = 0:49} | 0:10.00<br>0:10.50<br>0:11.00<br>0:11.75 |
| 2 | 10<br>(1,040 yards) | 80 | 1:3.75 | GP1 = 0:19.0<br>GP2 = 0:20.0<br>GP3 = 0:21.5<br>GP4 = 0:23.0 | 1:11<br>1:16<br>1:21<br>1:25 | (1 = 1:18)<br>[2 = 0:57]<br>{3 = 0:37} | 0:09.50<br>0:10.00<br>0:10.75<br>0:11.50 |
| 3 | 14<br>(1,456 yards) | 85 | 1:3.25 | GP1 = 0:18.5<br>GP2 = 0:19.5<br>GP3 = 0:21.0<br>GP4 = 0:22.0 | 1:00<br>1:04<br>1:08<br>1:11 | (1 = 1:06)<br>[2 = 0:45]<br>{3 = 0:25} | 0:09.25<br>0:09.75<br>0:10.50<br>0:11.00 |
| 4 | 16<br>(1,664 yards) | 90 | 1:2.75 | GP1 = 0:18.0<br>GP2 = 0:19.0<br>GP3 = 0:20.0<br>GP4 = 0:21.0 | 0:49<br>0:52<br>0:55<br>0:58 | (1 = 0:54)<br>[2 = 0:34]<br>{3 = 0:15} | 0:09.00<br>0:09.50<br>0:10.00<br>0:10.50 |

**VENUE:** *TENNIS COURT*

**DISTANCE:** *52-yard Long Shuttle*

| LEVEL | REPS<br>(TOTAL DISTANCE) | %<br>SPEED | W:R<br>RATIO | TARGET TIME | RECOVERY TIME | | RUN PACE<br>@ 26 YARDS |
|---|---|---|---|---|---|---|---|
| 1 | 10<br>(520 yards) | 80 | 1:5 | GP1 = 0:08.9<br>GP2 = 0:09.5<br>GP3 = 0:10.1<br>GP4 = 0:10.8 | 0:44<br>0:48<br>0:50<br>0:54 | (1 = 0:49)<br>[2 = 0:39]<br>{3 = 0:29} | 0:04.4<br>0:04.8<br>0:05.1<br>0:05.4 |
| 2 | 14<br>(728 yards) | 85 | 1:4.5 | GP1 = 0:08.6<br>GP2 = 0:09.2<br>GP3 = 0:09.8<br>GP4 = 0:10.4 | 0:39<br>0:41<br>0:44<br>0:47 | (1 = 0:43)<br>[2 = 0:33]<br>{3 = 0:24} | 0:04.3<br>0:04.6<br>0:04.9<br>0:05.2 |
| 3 | 18<br>(936 yards) | 90 | 1:4 | GP1 = 0:08.3<br>GP2 = 0:08.8<br>GP3 = 0:09.4<br>GP4 = 0:10.0 | 0:33<br>0:35<br>0:38<br>0:40 | (1 = 0:36)<br>[2 = 0:27]<br>{3 = 0:18} | 0:04.1<br>0:04.4<br>0:04.7<br>0:05.0 |
| 4 | 22<br>(1,144 yards) | 95 | 1:3.5 | GP1 = 0:07.9<br>GP2 = 0:08.5<br>GP3 = 0:09.0<br>GP4 = 0:09.6 | 0:28<br>0:30<br>0:32<br>0:34 | (1 = 0:31)<br>[2 = 0:22]<br>{3 = 0:13} | 0:04.0<br>0:04.2<br>0:04.5<br>0:04.8 |

# SHUTTLE RUN INTERVALS

**VENUE: VOLLEYBALL COURT**

**DISTANCE: 40-yard Side Shuttle**

| LEVEL | REPS (TOTAL DISTANCE) | % SPEED | W:R RATIO | TARGET TIME | RECOVERY TIME | | RUN PACE @ 20 YARDS |
|---|---|---|---|---|---|---|---|
| 1 | 10 (400 yards) | 80 | 1:5 | GP1 = 0:09.6<br>GP2 = 0:10.1<br>GP3 = 0:10.6<br>GP4 = 0:11.1 | 0:48<br>0:50<br>0:53<br>0:56 | (1 = 0:52)<br>[2 = 0:41]<br>{3 = 0:31} | 0:04.8<br>0:05.1<br>0:05.3<br>0:05.6 |
| 2 | 14 (560 yards) | 85 | 1:4.5 | GP1 = 0:09.4<br>GP2 = 0:09.8<br>GP3 = 0:10.3<br>GP4 = 0:10.8 | 0:42<br>0:44<br>0:46<br>0:49 | (1 = 0:45)<br>[2 = 0:35]<br>{3 = 0:25} | 0:04.7<br>0:04.9<br>0:05.2<br>0:05.4 |
| 3 | 20 (800 yards) | 90 | 1:4 | GP1 = 0:09.1<br>GP2 = 0:09.6<br>GP3 = 0:10.0<br>GP4 = 0:10.5 | 0:37<br>0:38<br>0:40<br>0:42 | (1 = 0:39)<br>[2 = 0:29]<br>{3 = 0:20} | 0:04.6<br>0:04.8<br>0:05.0<br>0:05.2 |
| 4 | 24 (960 yards) | 95 | 1:3.5 | GP1 = 0:08.9<br>GP2 = 0:09.3<br>GP3 = 0:09.7<br>GP4 = 0:10.2 | 0:31<br>0:33<br>0:34<br>0:36 | (1 = 0:33)<br>[2 = 0:24]<br>{3 = 0:14} | 0:04.5<br>0:04.7<br>0:04.9<br>0:05.1 |

**VENUE: VOLLEYBALL COURT**

**DISTANCE: 20-yard Side Shuttle**

| LEVEL | REPS (TOTAL DISTANCE) | % SPEED | W:R RATIO | TARGET TIME | RECOVERY TIME | | RUN PACE |
|---|---|---|---|---|---|---|---|
| 1 | 10 (200 yards) | 80 | 1:5 | GP1 = 0:4.2<br>GP2 = 0:4.4<br>GP3 = 0:4.7<br>GP4 = 0:4.9 | 0:21<br>0:22<br>0:23<br>0:25 | (1 = 0:23)<br>[2 = 0:18]<br>{3 = 0:14} | |
| 2 | 15 (300 yards) | 85 | 1:4.5 | GP1 = 0:4.1<br>GP2 = 0:4.3<br>GP3 = 0:4.5<br>GP4 = 0:4.8 | 0:18<br>0:19<br>0:20<br>0:21 | (1 = 0:20)<br>[2 = 0:15]<br>{3 = 0:11} | N.A. |
| 3 | 20 (400 yards) | 90 | 1:4 | GP1 = 0:4.0<br>GP2 = 0:4.2<br>GP3 = 0:4.4<br>GP4 = 0:4.6 | 0:16<br>0:17<br>0:18<br>0:18 | (1 = 0:17)<br>[2 = 0:13]<br>{3 = 0:09} | |
| 4 | 25 (500 yards) | 95 | 1:3.5 | GP1 = 0:3.8<br>GP2 = 0:4.0<br>GP3 = 0:4.2<br>GP4 = 0:4.5 | 0:13<br>0:14<br>0:15<br>0:16 | (1 = 0:14)<br>[2 = 0:10]<br>{3 = 0:06} | |

# SHUTTLE RUN INTERVALS

**VENUE:** **VOLLEYBALL COURT**

**DISTANCE:** **80-yard Long Shuttle**

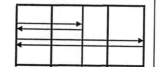

| LEVEL | REPS (TOTAL DISTANCE) | % SPEED | W:R RATIO | TARGET TIME | | RECOVERY TIME | | RUN PACE @ 40 YARDS |
|---|---|---|---|---|---|---|---|---|
| **1** | **8** (640 yards) | 77.5 | 1:4.5 | GP1 = 0:16.0 | 1:11 | (1 = 1:17) [2 = 1:00] {3 = 0:43} | | 0:08.00 |
| | | | | GP2 = 0:16.5 | 1:15 | | | 0:08.25 |
| | | | | GP3 = 0:17.5 | 1:20 | | | 0:08.75 |
| | | | | GP4 = 0:18.5 | 1:24 | | | 0:09.25 |
| **2** | **12** (960 yards) | 82.5 | 1:4 | GP1 = 0:15.5 | 1:01 | (1 = 1:07) [2 = 0:50] {3 = 0:33} | | 0:07.75 |
| | | | | GP2 = 0:16.0 | 1:05 | | | 0:08.00 |
| | | | | GP3 = 0:17.0 | 1:08 | | | 0:08.50 |
| | | | | GP4 = 0:18.0 | 1:12 | | | 0:09.00 |
| **3** | **16** (1,280 yards) | 87.5 | 1:3.5 | GP1 = 0:15.0 | 0:52 | (1 = 0:59) [2 = 0:40] {3 = 0:24} | | 0:07.50 |
| | | | | GP2 = 0:15.5 | 0:55 | | | 0:07.75 |
| | | | | GP3 = 0:16.5 | 0:58 | | | 0:08.25 |
| | | | | GP4 = 0:17.5 | 1:01 | | | 0:08.75 |
| **4** | **20** (1,600 yards) | 92.5 | 1:3 | GP1 = 0:14.5 | 0:43 | (1 = 0:47) [2 = 0:31] {3 = 0:16} | | 0:07.25 |
| | | | | GP2 = 0:15.0 | 0:45 | | | 0:07.50 |
| | | | | GP3 = 0:16.0 | 0:48 | | | 0:08.00 |
| | | | | GP4 = 0:17.0 | 0:51 | | | 0:08.50 |

**VENUE:** **VOLLEYBALL COURT**

**DISTANCE:** **60-yard Long Shuttle**

| LEVEL | REPS (TOTAL DISTANCE) | % SPEED | W:R RATIO | TARGET TIME | | RECOVERY TIME | | RUN PACE @ 30 YARDS |
|---|---|---|---|---|---|---|---|---|
| **1** | **10** (600 yards) | 80 | 1:5 | GP1 = 0:12.5 | 1:03 | (1 = 1:08) [2 = 0:55] {3 = 0:41} | | 0:06.25 |
| | | | | GP2 = 0:13.5 | 1:07 | | | 0:06.75 |
| | | | | GP3 = 0:14.0 | 1:10 | | | 0:07.00 |
| | | | | GP4 = 0:14.5 | 1:13 | | | 0:07.25 |
| **2** | **14** (840 yards) | 85 | 1:4.5 | GP1 = 0:12.0 | 0:55 | (1 = 1:00) [2 = 0:46] {3 = 0:33} | | 0:06.00 |
| | | | | GP2 = 0:13.0 | 0:58 | | | 0:06.50 |
| | | | | GP3 = 0:13.5 | 1:01 | | | 0:06.75 |
| | | | | GP4 = 0:14.0 | 1:04 | | | 0:07.00 |
| **3** | **18** (1,080 yards) | 90 | 1:4 | GP1 = 0:11.5 | 0:47 | (1 = 0:51) [2 = 0:39] {3 = 0:26} | | 0:05.75 |
| | | | | GP2 = 0:12.5 | 0:50 | | | 0:06.25 |
| | | | | GP3 = 0:13.5 | 0:53 | | | 0:06.50 |
| | | | | GP4 = 0:13.5 | 0:55 | | | 0:06.75 |
| **4** | **22** (1,320 yards) | 95 | 1:3.5 | GP1 = 0:11.0 | 0:40 | (1 = 0:43) [2 = 0:31] {3 = 0:19} | | 0:05.50 |
| | | | | GP2 = 0:12.0 | 0:42 | | | 0:06.00 |
| | | | | GP3 = 0:12.5 | 0:44 | | | 0:06.25 |
| | | | | GP4 = 0:13.0 | 0:47 | | | 0:06.50 |

# About the Authors

MATT BRZYCKI, B.S., is the Coordinator of Recreational Fitness and Wellness Programs at Princeton University in Princeton, New Jersey. He has more than 20 years of experience at the collegiate level as a coach, instructor and administrator. At Princeton University, Mr. Brzycki has also served as the Coordinator of Health Fitness, Strength and Conditioning Programs (1993-2001) and the Health Fitness Coordinator/Strength and Conditioning Coach (1990-93). Previously, he was an Assistant Strength and Conditioning Coach at Rutgers University (1984-90) and a Health Fitness Supervisor at Princeton University (1983-84). Mr. Brzycki earned his  Bachelor of Science degree in health and physical education from Penn State (1983). Prior to entering college, he served in the United States Marine Corps (1975-79). Mr. Brzycki has been a featured speaker at local, regional, state and national conferences and clinics throughout the United States and Canada. He has written more than 250 articles/columns on strength and fitness that have been featured in 40 different publications. Mr. Brzycki has authored, co-authored or edited 11 other books. In April 2004, he was appointed by the governor to serve as a member of the New Jersey Council on Physical Fitness and Sports. He and his wife, Alicia, reside in Lawrenceville, New Jersey, with their son, Ryan.

JASON GALLUCCI, M.S., is the Head Varsity Strength and Conditioning Coach at Princeton University in Princeton, New Jersey. He works with many of the school's 38 varsity teams, including women's basketball, field hockey, ice hockey, lacrosse, soccer and softball. Coach Gallucci is also the director of the Princeton University Strength & Speed Camp. Prior to his current position, he was an Assistant Strength and Conditioning Coach (for football) at Penn State (1998-2000). Coach Gallucci earned his Bachelor of Science degree in exercise and sports science (1997) and his Master of Science degree in biomechanics (kinesiology)

from Penn State (2000). He's a Certified Strength and Conditioning Specialist (CSCS) by the National Strength and Conditioning Association and a Strength and Conditioning Coach Certified (SCCC) by the Collegiate Strength and Conditioning Coaches Association. He and his wife, Angelique, reside in Lawrenceville, New Jersey, with their son, Jason Gabriel.

TOM KELSO, M.S., is the Coordinator, Strength & Conditioning at Saint Louis University in Saint Louis, Missouri. Coach Kelso works with all 18 men's and women's athletic teams. With more than 20 years of experience at the collegiate level, he has served as the Head Coach for Strength and Conditioning at the University of Illinois at Chicago (2001-04), Southeast Missouri State University (1991-2001) and the University of Florida (1988-90). At the University of Florida, he had been an Assistant Strength Coach (1984-88) and a weight-training instructor for the Department of Physical Education (1985-88). Coach Kelso received his Bachelor of Science degree in recreation education from the University of Iowa (1981) and his Master of Science degree in physical education from Western Illinois University (1984). While at Iowa, he was a member of the Track and Field Team; while at Western Illinois, he served as a Graduate Assistant Track and Field Coach. Coach Kelso is a Certified Strength and Conditioning Specialist (CSCS) by the National Strength and Conditioning Association (NSCA) and a Strength and Conditioning Coach Certified (SCCC) by the Collegiate Strength and Conditioning Coaches Association. In 2001, he received an honorary certification from the International Association of Resistance Trainers (IART). In 1999, Coach Kelso was named NSCA Ohio Valley Conference Strength and Conditioning Professional of the Year. A strong advocate of safe, practical and time-efficient training, he has authored numerous articles promoting such. Coach Kelso has worked with athletes at the Olympic and professional levels, presented at various clinics/seminars and has worked at several sport-related camps. He also serves on the Advisory Board of the IART.

SAM KNOPIK, M.Ed., is the Head Strength Coach and Football Coach at Pembroke Hill School in Kansas City, Missouri. Coach Knopik also teaches physical education and world history at the school. He earned his Bachelor of Arts degree in history from William Jewell College (1996) and his Master of Education degree in curriculum and instruction from the University of Missouri (1998). Coach Knopik co-authors a popular website (www.StrongerAthlete.com) that provides common-sense information on strength and conditioning for coaches and athletes. He and his wife, Sarah, reside in Liberty, Missouri, with their daughter, Emma.

JOHN RINALDO, B.S., is the owner and operator of a personal-training business (through Gold's Gym) in Worcester, Massachusetts. Previously, he was the Head Strength and Conditioning Coach at Providence College (1998-2002) where he helped the Friars basketball program earn a bid to the NCAA Tournament and two bids to the NIT. He also served as an Assistant Strength Coach for the Boston Celtics (1997-98), an Assistant Strength Coach at the University of Kentucky (1993-96) and the Head Strength Coach/Fitness Instructor at Lexington Catholic High School in Lexington, Kentucky (1994-96). Mr. Rinaldo received his Bachelor of Science degree in exercise science from the University of Kentucky (1996) and was a Masters candidate in the Exercise Science Graduate Program at The University of Massachusetts, Amherst (1996-98). He's a Certified Personal Trainer through The Aerobics and Fitness Association of America. Mr. Rinaldo is a contributing writer for *Pulse Magazine* and the Volunteer Public Relations Director for the Greater Worcester Special Olympics. Currently, he's pursuing an acting career that includes a role in the independent film *Freedom Park*.

SCOTT SAVOR, B.S., is the Head Strength/Conditioning Coach at University of Detroit Mercy in Detroit, Michigan. His duties include the implementation of strength and conditioning programs for the school's 16 varsity teams. Prior to his present position, Coach Savor was a member of the Strength and Conditioning Staff of the Minnesota Vikings (2000-2002), the Head Strength and Conditioning Coach at Shakopee High School (2001-2002) and a Fitness Specialist at a prestigious personalized training studio (Fitness First) in Chaska, Minnesota (2000-2002). He earned his Bachelor of Science degree in exercise science from Moorhead State University in Moorhead, Minnesota (2001). Coach Savor is pursuing a Master of Science degree in health services administration at the University of Detroit Mercy. Raised in Deerwood, Minnesota, he currently resides in Bloomfield Hills, Michigan.